D0661672

Leadership, Feedback
and the
Open Communication Gap

Leadership, Feedback
and the
Open Communication Gap

Leanne E. Atwater • David A. Waldman

Arizona State Univesity

 Lawrence Erlbaum Associates
Taylor & Francis Group

New York   London

BOWLING GREEN STATE
UNIVERSITY LIBRARY

Lawrence Erlbaum Associates
Taylor & Francis Group
270 Madison Avenue
New York, NY 10016

Lawrence Erlbaum Associates
Taylor & Francis Group
2 Park Square
Milton Park, Abingdon
Oxon OX14 4RN

© 2008 by Taylor & Francis Group, LLC
Lawrence Erlbaum Associates is an imprint of Taylor & Francis Group, an Informa business

Printed in the United States of America on acid-free paper
10 9 8 7 6 5 4 3 2 1

International Standard Book Number-13: 978-0-8058-5397-1 (Softcover) 978-0-8058-5396-4 (Hardcover)

Except as permitted under U.S. Copyright Law, no part of this book may be reprinted, reproduced, transmitted, or utilized in any form by any electronic, mechanical, or other means, now known or hereafter invented, including photocopying, microfilming, and recording, or in any information storage or retrieval system, without written permission from the publishers.

Trademark Notice: Product or corporate names may be trademarks or registered trademarks, and are used only for identification and explanation without intent to infringe.

Library of Congress Cataloging-in-Publication Data

Atwater, Leanne E.
    Leadership, feedback, and the open communication gap / Leanne E. Atwater and David A. Waldman.
        p. cm.
    Includes bibliographical references and index.
    ISBN 978-0-8058-5396-4 (alk. paper) -- ISBN 978-0-8058-5397-1 (alk. paper)
    1. Leadership. 2. Communication in management. 3. Employees--Rating of. I. Waldman, David A. (David Andrew), 1955- II. Title.

HD57.7.A83 2008
658.4'5--dc22
                                                                           2007037364

Visit the Taylor & Francis Web site at
http://www.taylorandfrancis.com

and the LEA and Routledge Web site at
http://www.routledge.com

This book is dedicated to my family, David, Sarah, Chelsea Atwater, and Stephanie, Jason and Zachary Walker for always making Sunday family dinner a #1 priority, and to Mom and Pop for their unconditional love. I love you all.

—Leanne Atwater

This book is dedicated to my loving parents, Ida and Lester Waldman. They continue to provide lifelong support and encouragement for my endeavors, and I will be forever grateful.

—David Waldman

Contents

List of Tables

Preface

It is our hope and desire that this book will be provocative for managers, researchers, and academics alike. The topic of leadership has grown in importance, and how and when managers communicate is critical to their effectiveness. We hope to provide specific insight into the topic of open communication and how it might become less of a dilemma for managers.

This project is born out of practice, research, and personal experience. In the literature and in our profession, we have heard many calls for open communication on the part of managers and organizations. However, in our own research, teaching, and consulting, we have observed and heard numerous examples of how open communication can pose dilemmas for people in leadership positions. For example, when we speak to our students and managers about the importance of sharing information with employees, on one level, they are likely to agree. Nevertheless, on another level, they have their doubts about the unequivocal practice of open communication in real-life settings.

Our targeted audiences are threefold. First, we provide insights for managers to understand the feedback and open communication processes. What outcomes and effects can be expected? How do characteristics of provider and recipient impact the open communication process? What are the dynamics of open communication in an upward direction? Second, we suggest guidelines for how and when managers should engage in negative feedback and open organizational-level communication with followers, including when such feedback and information should not be shared. In so doing, we serve one primary audience, specifically managers and practitioners involved in the practice of leadership.

Third, we add to the existing knowledge base pertaining to open communication on the part of managers as the contents of the book are largely research based. In the concluding chapter, we provide insights that should be helpful in guiding future research. As such, our work should be relevant to another primary audience, academics and students who are interested in open communication and leadership. Although the topic has been addressed in the literature, there is need for additional theory and research. We further believe our consideration of open communication at multiple levels of analysis can help provide a broader basis for theory and research to proceed. Open communication is not just a dilemma in one-on-one relationships; it is a leadership dilemma across the hierarchical levels of an organization, and for a broad array of information. We begin by discussing open communication and why it is a dilemma.

1

What Is Open Communication, and Why Is It a Dilemma?

Leadership is often heralded as essential for the ongoing revitalization of organizations. To be sure, revitalization is often critical. A myriad of factors have come together in recent times to threaten motivation, employee commitment and loyalty, and performance. These include downsizing, offshore outsourcing, acquisitions, and corporate scandals, to name just a few. Leadership is necessary to motivate and guide individuals, to transform groups of individuals into teams, and to provide a vision for the greater strategic direction of the organization. If leadership is a key basis for organizational performance, one can safely say communication is the key to effective leadership.

Communication permeates all aspects of leadership behavior. We see communication when a manager engages in one-on-one coaching with a subordinate. We see it in team meetings, when a manager attempts to get members to go beyond their differences and coalesce around a common goal. Furthermore, we see the importance of communication when a strategic manager meets with groups of individuals across an organization to garner ideas and build support for a new vision.

Much of what a manager communicates is positive and nonthreatening in nature. This is the relatively easy part of communication. Positively reinforcing work well done brings satisfaction to both the manager and the employee. Engaging in team problem solving can be intellectually stimulating to both manager and employees alike. Attempting to communicate and sell a vision can be challenging to the strategic manager, but at the same time, it can also be exhilarating, as more and more followers buy into the vision, thus making it shared.

However, there is another side to leadership communication that is much more troubling to managers and employees alike. It involves the presentation of information that is negative, threatening, or uncertain. As such, this information can cause hard feelings if communicated, or paradoxically, even if it is not communicated. The context can be one on one between a manager and an employee, or it can pertain to communication spread across hierarchical and functional levels. Either way, there is often a tendency to either consciously or unconsciously avoid the communication of negative information. Unfortunately, avoiding difficult issues rarely, if ever, makes them go away.

This is a book about open communication. We define open communication in terms of the difficult information potentially communicated by people in leadership positions, rather than the more positive or mundane information. When a manager spreads such information or perceptions to one or more individuals, he or she is communicating openly. As such, our focus is on the challenges or dilemmas these people face in being open communicators. The choices made will help determine whether they are ultimately seen as actual leaders, as opposed to people who are not fulfilling the leadership role. And as we will see, often the choices are not easy to make.

One theme of this book is that leadership communication is often paradoxical in nature. On the one hand, managers are barraged with advice to engage in frequent, open communication with followers. On the other hand, there is ample evidence to suggest caution in heeding this advice. Our goal is to use the findings from many studies in the research literature, as well as our personal experiences as feedback providers and recipients, consultants and professors, to help managers understand the complexities of the open communication paradox in order to be more effective in their roles.

THE ONE-ON-ONE DILEMMA: BEHAVIORAL AND PERFORMANCE FEEDBACK

In the first part of this book, we focus on the primary dilemmas managers face with regard to open, one-to-one communication or feedback. Society encourages us to give feedback to those around us. We tip servers at restaurants for good service, provide comments to hotel staff via customer surveys, speak with customer service representatives on the phone, and talk with mechanics at the auto garage about service issues. College students are encouraged to provide anonymous feedback to professors, and managers are encouraged to give honest performance appraisals to subordinates. At least in Western culture, we are encouraged to "tell it like it is," and "give it to them straight," thus being frank and honest in our dealings with others.

In a work context, the focus of feedback has traditionally been in the downward direction from bosses to subordinates. This feedback could be formal appraisal feedback with salary or other outcomes associated with it, or more informal feedback suggesting how the subordinate is doing in his or her job. In many cases, the feedback is positive, and the subordinate perceives the feedback as positive recognition or rewarding. Positive feedback tends to motivate the recipient, and in general, it has positive outcomes (Jaworski & Kohli, 1991; Korsgaard, 1996).

Unfortunately, the same cannot be said for negative feedback. Yet, much of the feedback an individual (including a manager) needs to deliver to others, in a variety of contexts, is not positive, such as when absenteeism, performance problems, attitude problems, and the like arise. Often delivery of negative feedback is delayed, handled inappropriately, or avoided altogether. Managers often report transmitting negative feedback to subordinates as one of their most unpleasant and difficult tasks (Larson, 1984, 1986; Veiga, 1988). They also report that they avoid giving negative feedback until annoyance is very high, and then it is often harsh and punishing (Larson, 1989).

Learning theories suggest we can shape behavior depending on the type of reinforcement we provide to others. Positive reinforcement in the form of positive feedback should encourage more behavior; punishment in the form of negative feedback should encourage less behavior. However, punishment does not always result in less unwanted behavior, and it is often accompanied by unwanted side effects (Atwater, Waldman, Carey, & Cartier, 2001). Similarly, negative feedback does not always result in positive behavior change and may be accompanied by a variety of negative side effects. Indeed, in many cases, there is evidence that feedback does not result in positive outcomes. Kluger and DeNisi (1996) conducted a meta-analysis analyzing hundreds of feedback studies. They concluded that feedback decreased performance in one third of the cases, had no effect on performance in one third of the cases, and improved performance in one third of the cases. Their analysis included both positive and negative feedback interventions. Based on the results of studies that compared positive and negative feedback (e.g., Jaworski & Kohli, 1991), we can speculate that if only negative feedback had been provided, the cases of improvement would have been reduced still further.

In the first part of this book the focus is on the dilemmas associated with negative feedback. We discuss reactions managers can expect to different types of feedback and different methods of delivery. We also discuss how individual characteristics of both the feedback provider and recipient can influence the interaction and its outcomes. In addition, the manager as feedback recipient is also addressed.

For a person in a leadership role, giving feedback is essential but receiving feedback, whether positive or negative, also is considered essential to developing a sense of self-awareness and realistic self-perceptions. Pity goes to the manager who lacks self-awareness of his or her own strengths and weaknesses. Furthermore, self-awareness is an important aspect of emotional intelligence (the ability of people to understand and manage their personal feelings and emotions toward others) and is the key to self-regulation, both of which are crucial to effective leadership (Ashford & Tsui, 1991; Daft, 2002). Thus, feedback should be considered a primary source of leadership development. Although our primary focus in this book is on the manager as feedback provider, the manager as feedback recipient is also addressed.

Case Example

Kathy worked in a job setting where she was one of the least qualified, in terms of experience and credentials, among her peers. Her manager hired Kathy primarily because she was a good friend of another manager in the organization. Her performance was generally mediocre, although not unsatisfactory.

To help Kathy develop her skills, the manager asked a task group working on a special project to include her as one of their members. The task group generally liked Kathy as a person and agreed to do so. Over the next few months, the task group came to believe that Kathy lacked both the ability and motivation to be a productive group member. The contributions she tried to make to the group's task were rarely helpful. Furthermore, she arrived late to meetings or missed them entirely, and her attitude toward the group members was rather negative. Kathy also had a rather low sense of self-confidence and had a reputation for being confrontational at times.

The task group decided that they could not be productive with Kathy as a member. Her poor contributions, poor attitude, and apparent lack of motivation were disrupting the dynamics and productivity of the group. The task group contemplated how to deal with the situation. Ultimately, they decided they would meet with her as a group, provide feedback to her about their perceptions of her contributions (which might have been due to a lack of effort or interest), and her apparent negative attitude toward group members. They would then ask Kathy whether she wanted to try to modify her behavior and put more effort into the group, or whether she thought it best to leave the group. They were acting with the best of intentions, attempting to be honest with Kathy. After all, isn't feedback always a good thing?

Analysis

Maybe feedback is not always a good thing. In this situation, the feedback meeting turned out to be a disaster. The short-term outcome was shouting, name calling, and tears among some group members, especially Kathy. The long-term outcomes included ruined relationships among Kathy, the task group members, and the manager who asked the group to include her. As an example, Kathy would simply not speak to certain members for weeks following the meeting.

So what went wrong in this case? Clearly there were a number of factors that contributed to the negative outcomes. These included Kathy's personal characteristics, relationships among the players (including the manager), status differences, the manner in which the feedback was delivered, the content of the feedback, and so forth. Could the feedback have been delivered in a more productive way, or should feedback have been avoided entirely? We revisit this case in a later chapter.

If feedback is supposed to be sought by employees, provided by managers, and heeded by employees in making improvements, we are in need of a much better understanding of when, how, and to whom feedback should be given. Providing advice to managers and employees about how to deal with these types of decisions regarding feedback (whether, how, what, and when) constitutes much of the focus of this book.

THE ORGANIZATIONAL DILEMMA: INFORMATION SHARING ACROSS LEVELS

The second dilemma we address in the second part of the book deals with the issue of sharing information across hierarchical levels and functional areas of an organization. As such, this dilemma is much broader than the first one, which is more focused on one-on-one feedback. The second dilemma deals with communication across an entire organization. Despite this difference there are important similarities—and problems—both types of leadership communication share.

Managerial role taxonomies generally include aspects of open communication across hierarchical levels and functional areas. Early work by Mintzberg (1973) included the disseminator role. Mintzberg stressed that relevant information must be passed along by managers to employees, either in its unadulterated, original form or after interpretation and editing by the manager. Similarly, Yukl (2002) stressed the importance of the informing role, especially under crisis or uncertain situations. The following quote from Daft (2002) is representative of the common thinking in the literature regarding the open sharing of information across levels: "Open communication improves the operations of a company, builds trust, spreads knowledge, and provides a foundation for communicating vision, values, and other vital big-picture information" (p. 322).

The feeling, which is certainly quite intuitive, is that one cannot have too much communication in an organization. Those espousing unfettered, open communication believe management knowledge and information should, in essence, constitute an open book (Dalton, 1999; Pfeffer & Veiga, 1999). If it is good enough for upper management to know, then it is also good enough for those at the lower levels to know, especially if the information is in some way relevant to those individuals. Peters (1987) is perhaps the most ardent supporter of open-book communication. He went so far as to say "information distortion" and secrecy constitute "management enemy number one" (p. 513).

The proponents of open communication would point to logical outcomes. If upper management shares information with employees at lower levels, trust should permeate the organization, thus inspiring collaboration and commitment to common goals (Martin, 1998; McCune, 1998). Second, open communication should foster a feeling of employee ownership regarding organizational goals and challenges. Third, if upper level managers serve as role models for open communication, we should expect those at lower levels to reciprocate. That is, when managers openly communicate, lower level employees will be more inclined to share information in an upward manner, allowing executives to better understand their organizations and make more informed decisions.

Unfortunately, it is not so simple. To better understand the leadership dilemma of information sharing across levels, it is necessary to delineate the types of information shared, but that is also potentially difficult, negative, threatening, or uncertain. Although numerous examples could be imagined, we identify some common ones here. First, there is the issue of sharing information about a planned or potential organizational restructuring (e.g., downsizing). Second, there is the issue of relaying information to lower levels regarding potential merger or acquisition developments. Third, there is the question of whether or not policy or procedural changes should be communicated to people at lower levels that might interest them, but might not be directly relevant to their work. For example, should changes in executive compensation practices be communicated to lower level employees?

Case Example

Harmony, Inc. (fictitious name) is a producer and distributor of a growing product line of naturally processed foods. The company prides itself in making foods with all-natural ingredients and a minimum of processing in their production. Their foods are sold primarily in natural food stores and groceries.

The company employs approximately 2,000 individuals and is based in Phoenix, Arizona. It was founded 25 years ago by a small group of partners and is still a private firm, resisting opportunities in the past to go public. The original partners were strong believers in corporate social responsibility values, including respect for the natural environment, helping to feed the homeless, and maintaining a healthy work environment for its employees. Part of the latter includes the maintenance of open communication with employees on a wide range of issues facing management and the organization.

Recently, officials of Dynamic Foods, Inc. (fictitious name) approached the founding partners of Harmony, Inc. with a takeover proposition. Dynamic Foods is a large, publicly traded food processing company based out of Chicago. It has noticed trends in the marketplace toward naturally processed foods and would like to gain a foothold into this market. Accordingly, the acquisition of Harmony, Inc. seemed attractive. In addition, Dynamic Foods would be able to gain technical knowledge about the processing of natural foods, which could be beneficial for their main operations.

The initial proposition seemed interesting to the partners of Harmony, Inc. The majority of them had been recently considering retirement, and the initial offer from Dynamic Foods appeared to be quite promising. It appeared with some work, a deal might be negotiated. However, a number of issues would need to be worked out. For example, there was some desire on the part of a few of the Harmony, Inc. partners to be placed on the board of directors of Dynamic Foods for the purpose of ensuring the continuation of corporate social responsibility for the Harmony, Inc. portion of the new entity in particular, and the greater firm in general.

In line with their open communication culture, the partners gave the green light to the upper management of Harmony, Inc. to communicate down the hierarchy about the takeover negotiations. Employees were told Dynamic Foods was interested in Harmony, Inc. purely for synergistic reasons (e.g., to be able to quickly get into the natural foods market). Employees were assured that the negotiations would include a consideration of the company's corporate social responsibility values, as well as employee relations and needs. Employees were also asked not to "make a big deal" out of the negotiations (e.g., go to the media) because they were only tentative and exploratory.

Unfortunately, a number of lower level managers and employees did make a big deal out of the situation. Soon after the announcement of the negotiations, the organizational grapevine heated up. Employees lamented among each other about how Dynamic Foods was just another large corporate producer of processed foods. To many, it was a company that cared little about its customers or its employees. Information was spread around about how Dynamic Foods had taken over another company several years ago, and the result was massive layoffs at the acquired firm. Moreover, Dynamic Foods cared little about corporate social responsibility and would just use the resources at Harmony to improve their bottom line. Further, despite the claims of Dynamic Foods about pursuing synergies with Harmony as the basis for the acquisition, a rumor was spread about the executives of Dynamic Foods really just wanting to have an excuse to visit Phoenix in the winter for the purpose of lavish, golf-playing junkets.

Several employees of Harmony, Inc. even decided to go to the local media in Phoenix to talk about their fears and the potential negative impact on the community (e.g., likely layoffs at the firm). The result was a not-so-flattering article in the local newspaper about the possible deal, as well as negative coverage by a local television station.

Of course, officials at Dynamic Foods found out about the media coverage. This coverage, coupled with angry letters from some employees of Harmony, Inc., caused the tone of the acquisition negotiations to go from collaborative to confrontational quite quickly. Officials from Dynamic Foods accused the Harmony, Inc. partners and executives of, at best, being too loose with sensitive information, and at worst, seeking to spoil the negotiations. On their part, the partners and executives of Harmony, Inc. accused the Dynamic Foods officials of being less than straightforward about their true intentions, insinuating some of the rumors spreading around among their employees might be true.

It should not be surprising that after several weeks, the negotiations reached an impasse and were suspended. In the continued spirit of open communication, the partners and executives of Harmony, Inc. went back to the organization and announced there would be no further negotiations with Dynamic Foods. They hoped things would return to normal. Unfortunately, in the weeks and months following the suspended negotiations, there seemed to be negative fallout at Harmony, Inc. In short, things were not so "harmonized." Employee morale seemed to have suffered, and there was less trust in management and their intentions. If they had negotiated with Dynamic Foods to have the firm acquired, why would they not negotiate with other firms for similar deals? Was the firm on an inevitable course toward being absorbed by mainstream corporate America, with little concern for the welfare of employees or the greater society?

Analysis

What went wrong in this particular case? Was open communication clearly the right strategy for Harmony, Inc. to use with its employees? It could be argued that open communication was indeed appropriate, but perhaps management did not go far enough. That is, perhaps more information should have been shared about the parameters of the negotiations (e.g., the partners' attempts to serve on the board of the newly created entity). However, another argument could be made for information secrecy. Based on such an argument, the partners and management at Harmony, Inc. should not have shared information about the negotiations with Dynamic Foods, at least not until those negotiations were closer to being consummated. Obviously, such an argument flies in the face of the principle of open leadership communications. Yet, as we report in a later chapter, such information secrecy is the norm in the context of merger and acquisition negotiations. We also discuss in a later chapter the factors managers need to consider in deciding what information and how much information should be shared with employees, when to share, and the optimal delivery methods for different types of communications.

To summarize, the open communication of organizational-level information is indeed a dilemma for managers. It makes intuitive sense, and it fits in neatly with organizational cultural trends emphasizing collaboration, openness, and trust building across hierarchical levels and functional divides. Nevertheless, we are in need of a much better understanding of when, how, and with whom such information should be shared. A major goal of this book is to provide insight for managers about how to deal with the dilemma of open communication in their organizations under various circumstances. We address conditions under which open communication is clearly warranted versus contexts in which managers might want to refrain from being so open.

The Open Communication Dilemma in One-to-One Communication

2

Performance Feedback and Its Effects

Feedback is encouraged in organizations because it is expected to improve self-awareness and can be used to modify behavior (e.g., improve performance, fix behavior problems). Feedback is also useful to motivate or direct employees or to reinforce desired behavior. However, because not all feedback is positive, it might not be well received for a variety of reasons. For example, feedback recipients might react in ways that can diminish or eliminate its positive effects. Worse yet, feedback can also result in reactions having deleterious effects on performance, attitudes, or both. As such, feedback, although an example of open communication, is not always effective or desirable. In this chapter, we explore the "dark side" of feedback, and how research shows it can present a dilemma for managers in organizations. This chapter highlights research that has looked at various types of feedback and the reactions and outcomes managers can expect. We also highlight personal experiences and some suggestions for improving outcomes.

Geddes and Baron (1997) reported that in over half of the cases in which employees were given negative feedback, their performance declined. Atwater, Waldman, et al. (2001) studied discipline delivery, much of which took the form of oral corrective feedback. That study, which included interviews with 123 people who had been disciplined or received corrective feedback, revealed that recipients reported improvements in only half of the incidents (e.g., problem performance improved, greater clarification of expectations, problem solved). However, there were also often negative effects on attitudes and relationships with supervisors. That is, recipients reported that they were unhappy (e.g., "I was crying," "I was upset"), angry ("I was outraged that they were doing this," "I was livid," "I was ticked off," "It made me very angry and I went out and

sought other employment"), or embarrassed ("Whenever you do something that is wrong and you know it is wrong, you feel embarrassed").
They also often reported that the relationship between the recipient and
the supervisor who delivered the feedback deteriorated. For example, one
individual reported, "The negative outcome is this whole feeling when
I see her ... now I have no respect." The conclusions from the study were
"clearly most recipients, even if they accepted responsibility for their
behavior and felt that the punishment was fair had negative emotional
reactions to the discipline" (Atwater, Waldman, et al., 2001, pp. 262,
264, 265). So, we begin this chapter with what seems to be a feedback
paradox. Although the open communication of feedback information is
seemingly important, its actual implementation seems problematic. The
next section highlights some of the reactions managers can expect if they
provide criticism or negative feedback.

REACTIONS TO FEEDBACK

Negative Emotions

Anger is a relatively common reaction individuals have to negative
feedback (Atwater, Carey, & Waldman, 2001; Fehr, Baldwin, Collins,
Patterson, & Benditt, 1999). Atwater and Brett (2005) found that
negative feedback from direct reports as part of a 360-degree feedback
process was related to emotions such as anger, unhappiness, discouragement, and disappointment. Atwater, Carey, and Waldman (2001)
reported that roughly 40% of the recipients expressed anger following a disciplinary incident directed at them. Although anger might be
expected to characterize men's reactions to negative feedback more
often than women's reactions, given the stereotypes of male dominance
and female passivity, their research found that men and women did not
differ in the extent to which they felt anger in response to negative
feedback. What was interesting, however, was the impact the gender of
the supervisor had on these reactions. Roughly 30% of men and 30% of
women reported feeling angry when a male supervisor delivered negative feedback; however, 50% of men and 58% of women reported feeling
angry when a female supervisor delivered discipline. Follow-up analyses
showed this effect could not be attributed to more harsh feedback being
delivered by women. In fact, if anything, women delivered less harsh
feedback. The authors speculated that the greater anger expressed
toward women had to do with the different gender role expectations
employees have for male and female supervisors. We explore these and
other gender effects in greater detail later in chapter 3.

Rudawsky, Lundgren, and Grasha (1999) found the more negative
the feedback, the more recipients reacted with competitive verbal
aggression. This finding suggests that it is not merely negative feedback
in any form, but rather the more negative the feedback, the more severe

the negative reaction might be. In the Atwater, Waldman, et al. (2001) study, one recipient reported (tongue in cheek), "Murder came to mind; things like that" (p. 264). Others reported becoming bitter toward the supervisor or intent on seeking revenge. A sample comment was "I was ticked off, seeking revenge and then I slashed my boss's tires." Some of this anger seems to result from perceptions about the feedback being unfair, or unfairly harsh, and might be mitigated by the way the feedback is delivered. In some cases managers think they need to seem very harsh and tough to get the employee's attention. We would suggest rethinking this, particularly if the employee has not received negative feedback about the issue previously.

Self-Esteem and Self-Efficacy

Negative feedback also has been shown to result in decreased self-efficacy among feedback recipients. Self-efficacy is a task-specific belief in one's ability to perform in a particular situation. Further, individuals report lower estimates of their ability to perform in the future after receiving negative feedback (McCarty, 1986). If negative feedback reduces self-efficacy, it will also likely reduce individuals' motivation to make improvements following negative feedback, as they are less likely to believe their efforts will be successful (Bandura, 1986).

Although negative feedback may lower motivation, self-efficacy, and self-confidence, the extent to which it has a negative impact depends in part on the cause to which the individual attributes the performance failure. Silver, Mitchell, and Gist (1995) found that individuals with lower self-efficacy were more likely to attribute performance failure to themselves and their poor ability, a finding contrary to the self-serving bias (i.e., individuals tend to accept responsibility for their successes and deny responsibility for their failures; Heider, 1958). Conversely, individuals with high self-efficacy were more likely to attribute the failure to bad luck, a finding in line with the self-serving bias.

Individuals with high self-esteem also often do not react to negative feedback in a constructive way. McFarlin and Blascovich (1981) found that individuals with high self-esteem predicted their future performance to be better after they received failure feedback, as compared to individuals who received success feedback. This could indicate defensiveness and a need to present themselves favorably to others (i.e., compensatory self-enhancement; Baumeister & Jones, 1978). It is also consistent with the idea that those with high self-esteem have a greater need for approval than those with modest self-esteem (Kimble & Helmreich, 1972). This is somewhat surprising, as it would seem individuals with high self-esteem should not need the approval of others. However, it is consistent with suggestions by Kimble and Helmreich (1972) that individuals with moderate self-esteem are most well adjusted. It might be important for supervisors to be sensitive to the need for approval by those with high self-esteem. Perhaps supervisors need to allow those with high self-esteem to save face by providing some positive feedback before negative feedback.

If supervisors need to give negative feedback to individuals who are high in self-esteem, it is particularly important for individuals with high self-esteem to have respect for their supervisors. Fedor, Davis, Maslyn, and Mathieson (2001) found that self-reported intentions to improve performance following negative feedback for those with high self-esteem were much higher if the recipients believed their supervisor had high referent power (based on admiration and respect), as compared to when they believed the supervisor had low referent power. For those with low self-esteem, the supervisor's referent power was not highly relevant. Again, this might be a signal that those with lower self-esteem are more willing to accept negative feedback. For those with high self-esteem, it is likely to only be considered if the individual has a great deal of respect for the supervisor who is delivering the feedback.

Kluger and DeNisi (1996) also discussed the issue of internal versus external attribution for the problem; that is, is the failure or problem a person is being given negative feedback about the result of something within the individual (lack of ability or motivation) or is the failure due, at least in part, to the characteristics of the environment or situation? They suggested in the face of negative feedback, an internal attribution for the cause of failure might result in the individual disengaging from the task. However, if paired with cues fostering high self-efficacy, attention might be directed back to the task and lead people to invest in improvements. It does seem from this study that even if the manager "flies off the handle" and impulsively reacts to an infraction (or multiple infractions), to some extent the negative reactions of the recipient can be "saved," if the manager can later instill in the recipient confidence in his or her ability to improve.

There thus seems to be a circular pattern here. Negative feedback results in lower self-efficacy for those whose self-efficacy is already low because it is additional feedback to them that they are incapable. High-self-efficacy individuals are more resilient to the negative feedback because they are able to attribute the negative feedback to factors outside their ability. In sum, it appears that giving negative feedback to those with low self-efficacy will further reduce their opinions of themselves and lower their motivation and performance expectations. Negative feedback to those with high self-efficacy will not deter their motivation or performance expectations, but it also does little to improve their degree of self-awareness about their actual abilities. So although we would like negative feedback to alter the individual's level of self-awareness toward greater awareness ("Gee, maybe I'm not as good at this as I thought I was") and motivate the individual to improve, this might not always be the case. Again, elements of the feedback delivery process might be able to reduce the negative fallout on self-confidence and improve the attention paid to feedback by those with high self-confidence.

Individuals' perceptions of their inherent abilities also can be influenced by feedback. Zhou (1998) provided artificial positive or negative feedback to individuals about their creativity. That is, the feedback did not really reflect the creativity in their responses. Subsequently, those who received the artificial negative feedback were less creative in their ideas than those who received the positive artificial feedback. This could be evidence of the self-fulfilling prophecy in which individuals live up to the expectations others have set for them whether those expectations are realistic or not (Eden, 1984; Eden et al., 2000). As such, we can look at this example as suggesting positive feedback, even when it is not warranted, might increase performance because the individual sets higher expectations for himself or herself. Likewise, negative feedback, whether or not warranted, might cause individuals to have lower confidence of success and to set lower expectations, resulting in decreased performance.

Positive feedback generally is shown to have positive effects as noted in the two preceding examples. This might be especially true for those who provide low evaluations of themselves. Korsgaard (1996) found that individuals who provided low self-appraisals were more motivated by positive feedback than those who provided high self-ratings. Based on Korsgaard's results, when disagreement between self-appraisals and appraisals by others results from severely low self-ratings, feedback is more likely to have a positive effect, probably because it is motivating. This study also suggested that self- and supervisor ratings in the appraisals can result in differential effects of the feedback, depending on the nature of the self-appraisal. For those who find the feedback higher than self-ratings, the feedback is positive and motivational. However, for those who find the feedback lower than self-ratings, it is neither positive nor motivational. This suggests a valuable use for self-appraisals. Managers will have awareness of whether the individual has highly overrated himself or herself and whether negative feedback will therefore be less likely to be effective.

Silver, Conte, Miceli, and Poggi (1986) suggested the following with regard to self-efficacy and providing negative feedback: To encourage the development of strong efficacy beliefs, managers need to be careful about the way negative feedback is delivered. Criticism by managers that attributes the cause of poor performance to internal factors reduces the individual's confidence in his or her abilities and therefore his or her self-set goals are low (Baron, 1988, 1990). Managers should encourage people who are performing poorly to exert more effort or to develop better strategies. If an ability deficit is the primary cause of poor performance, managers should encourage their subordinates to learn from their mistakes. Although the effect of a single statement is not likely to exert much influence on self-efficacy beliefs, the patterns of verbal information given over time will impact people's perceptions of their capabilities (Bandura, 1986; Silver et al., 1986).

Stajkovic and Luthans (1998) also provided the following suggestions to minimize the negative impact on self-efficacy: (a) Managers

TABLE 2.1   Lessons Learned: Self-Esteem and Self-Efficacy

Low Self-Esteem	High Self-Esteem	Low Self-Efficacy	High Self-Efficacy
More open to negative feedback but might further reduce self-esteem	Tend to ignore negative feedback	Be sure negative feedback does not reflect lack of ability; individual must feel capable of improvement	Blame unsuccessful performance on outside factors
Maintaining confidence in ability is important	Individuals have high need for approval	Individuals take personal responsibility for negative feedback	Need to clearly show how individual's behavior resulted in outcomes
	Sandwich negative feedback with positive	Clear directives important	
		Provide positive feedback whenever possible	

need to provide clear, accurate descriptions of tasks employees are being asked to perform to increase their chances of successful performance; and (b) managers should help employees cope with complex tasks and teach them that ability is an incremental skill. If ability is perceived as a given entity, mistakes are perceived as an indication of the individual's intellectual capacity, which implies a lack of control (Bandura, 1991). The perceived lack of control leads to personal anxiety (Thompson, 1981), which in turn diminishes learning and ultimately results in reduced self-efficacy for future performance.

Obviously, it is also important, whenever possible, to provide positive feedback about successful performance to enhance self-efficacy. Managers clearly need to try to avoid lowering self-efficacy, but positive results will be seen when self-efficacy can be enhanced. Table 2.1 summarizes the lessons regarding self-esteem and self-efficacy.

Perceptions of Accuracy and Usefulness

So why exactly is there typically such a troubling reaction to negative feedback? Studies have shown negative feedback is likely to be perceived as less accurate and less useful than positive feedback (cf. Brett &

Atwater, 2001; Rudawsky et al., 1999). Feedback perceived as inaccurate or not useful is unlikely to be taken seriously or used to modify one's self-awareness or future behavior. Self-enhancement theory (cf. Brown, 1986) suggests that individuals are motivated to see themselves positively or favorably. Negative feedback detracts from this positive self-view. As such, individuals might attempt to avoid situations in which they will be unsuccessful or they might interpret negative feedback in a distorted way in an attempt to maintain their positive self-perception. It requires a balance to present feedback in such a way so it is not discounted and it does not result in reduced self-efficacy. One such approach is to pair negative feedback with positive feedback in other areas of the individual's performance. For example the manager might say, "Chet, you have been a very loyal employee and I appreciate your excellent attendance record. I truly value employees like you. But I have to caution you about leaving the doors unlocked two nights this week. This has serious consequences for our security. I'm sure after this reminder in the future you will be conscientious about checking the doors before you leave."

OUTCOMES OF POSITIVE AND NEGATIVE FEEDBACK

In addition to negative individual reactions, the overall conclusion is that although supervisors and managers often must deliver negative feedback, it is often ineffective and does not have its intended effects on individual and organizational outcomes. In this section, we discuss the potential outcomes of positive and negative feedback.

Conflict

Increased degrees of conflict have also been shown to result from negative feedback (Peterson, 1983). These conflicts generally arise between the feedback provider and the feedback recipient. They can erupt during feedback delivery in terms of argument or displays of anger. The recipient might disagree with the feedback and believe it is incorrect. As such, it is important for the feedback provider to have as much factual documentation for the negative feedback as possible. It is also important for the feedback provider to allow the recipient to share his or her thoughts and to avoid getting angry or defensive with the recipient. It is easy to see how a discussion could turn into a shouting match if the feedback provider allows such a thing to happen.

Conflict over negative feedback also might generalize to others in the workplace. For example, on receiving a negative performance appraisal, individuals might look to their peers to see if they, too, received negative appraisals. If the recipient perceives his or her appraisal (feedback) was unwarranted or unfair compared to the appraisals others received, this can lead to increased conflict among peers. In this instance, principles of equity, which are perceptions of fairness that individuals have when they compare the ratio of their inputs to outcomes with those of others, have been violated. When the situation is perceived as inequitable, motivation decreases, and conflict between the recipient and his or her comparators is likely to arise. At least in a Western cultural context, it is important to have documentation and objective assessments to the extent possible in an attempt to alter the recipient's perceptions. We discuss potential cultural issues and complications to open communication in later chapters.

Performance

Most of the evidence that negative feedback has a positive effect on performance has been based on contrived laboratory studies using very simple tasks and undergraduate student subjects (cf. Bandura & Cervone, 1983; Podsakoff & Farh, 1989). In one of the few field experiments done on feedback effects, Waldersee and Luthans (1994) studied negative feedback in relation to customer service performance among fast-food employees. Employees were given either positive or corrective feedback based on their interactions with customers. They were followed for 3 weeks. Feedback effects were assessed by comparing pre- and postfeedback customer service quality. Those in the corrective feedback group did not improve any more than those in a control group receiving no feedback, although they did improve more than the group that received positive feedback. That is, in this context, positive feedback had a more negative effect on performance than negative feedback. Waldersee and Luthans concluded that corrective feedback was unsuccessful in improving customer service performance, although they noted that the nature of the task (i.e., routine, simple, well mastered) in this study should be seriously considered. It seems in routine tasks, and when opportunities for goal setting and self–other comparisons are rare, feedback seems to be less successful. The fact that positive feedback did not result in improvements in this setting might be due, in part, to the type of job being done and this is discussed in a subsequent chapter.

Absenteeism

Arvey and Jones (1985) studied the impact of positive and negative feedback on absenteeism. When positive behavior (e.g., good attendance) received positive reinforcement (i.e., privileges) and excessive absenteeism was punished with progressive discipline, substantial reductions in absenteeism were realized. However, when punishment was used to control absenteeism without positive reinforcement, absenteeism increased. It seems punishment alone was interpreted by recipients as management's attempt to clamp down and was thus resisted.

Job Satisfaction

Numerous leadership studies have demonstrated that managers who use a management by exception-active style (looking for mistakes and pointing them out) have subordinates who report lower job satisfaction (Bass, 1990b). Few employees want to go to work dreading the sound of their supervisor's footsteps because it means he or she has found a mistake or a problem with their work. "Criticism from superior to subordinate tends to function ineffectively or negatively" (Cederblom, 1982, p. 225). Cederblom (1982) reported that decreased job satisfaction and reduced improvements have occurred as a result of supervisors' uses of criticism. However, Cederblom also reported that criticism in the form of explicit fair warning about misbehavior or poor performance can be appropriate and just. Thus, for the purpose of being an effective open communicator, the supervisor might need to report to the employee that his or her performance levels are not satisfactory, and if they do not improve, the employee will not be rewarded or even retained by the organization. Miner (1975) recommended, even though criticism is generally ineffective, that criticism in the form of warning the subordinate about problem behavior or inadequate performance is needed. It is certainly advisable to give an employee fair warning and a chance to improve rather than merely continuing to document a problem without sharing it with the employee.

Improvements Over Time

There is also research suggesting improvements resulting from frequent corrective feedback are unlikely to be sustained over time because individuals abandon their internal standards (Campion & Lord, 1982). In essence, they become desensitized to the feedback. Instead of reflecting on their performance and whether it meets their own set standards for performance, they come to rely on the external feedback they receive. In addition, because it often provides no new information ("My number of answered calls was lower than desired again … so what's new"), it provides little motivational value, except perhaps in motivating the employee to look for another job. So perhaps negative feedback delivery operates similarly to positive feedback in terms of the schedules of delivery. Those studying behavior shaping indicate that behavior is maintained over a long period of time when variable schedules of positive reinforcement are used. Variable schedules are unpredictable; that is, the individual does not know exactly when he or she will receive a reward. Because the reward cannot be predicted, behavior is maintained for a long period of time in waiting for the next reward. It appears that negative reinforcement or negative feedback might operate on a similar schedule; that is, it might be more effective when it is not constant and individuals are worried about when it might be delivered. Constant feedback, positive or negative, might soon be ignored.

Case Example

Frank is a 62-year-old veteran employee of Triple Creek Paper Company. He is a senior sales associate, assigned to one of the best territories in the state. Frank's performance has been good over the years, but not as good as he thinks. Whenever awards are provided for stellar performance, Frank believes he deserves them. One could say his self-esteem and self-efficacy regarding his sales performance are quite high. Recently, the organization has undergone some serious financial problems and, as a result, territories have been expanded and some associates have been let go. Frank was kept on, in part, due to his long tenure and his upcoming eligibility for retirement. Frank, due to his inflated beliefs in his excellent performance, is unaware he was even considered for an early retirement proposal.

Performance standards at Triple Creek Paper Company have recently been raised. Whereas a number of years ago, hitting 80% of your sales target was acceptable and hitting 90% even resulted in a small bonus, now no bonuses were being awarded for any performance below 100% of target. This quarter, Frank's performance was 92% of his sales target. As a result, Frank's district manager let Frank know his sales had not reached their target and unfortunately he would not be receiving a bonus this quarter.

Frank had been a proponent of the increased sales targets when they were discussed earlier in the year, and it seemed to his supervisor that he had taken the news well. However, after leaving the meeting with his supervisor, Frank had time to reconsider and sent a nasty e-mail to his supervisor indicating how disappointed he was that the supervisor had not taken into account all of his prior years of excellent performance, as well as the fact that he had sold some products lagging in the market. He was extremely disappointed that his supervisor had not awarded him the bonus, even though he had not exactly met the criteria. Frank, of course, did not believe others who had not met the target deserved the bonus. In this case, Frank attributed his lack of bonus to the poor judgment of his supervisor and his supervisor's lack of consideration of other factors in Frank's performance.

Analysis

Frank has a very high sense of self-esteem. He is not very receptive to any type of negative feedback. Instead, he makes an external attribution that it is his supervisor's poor judgment that resulted in his lack of bonus, rather than the fact that he just did not meet the sales target. We discuss the optimal way to handle this situation in an upcoming chapter.

THE FEEDBACK PARADOX

The problems concerning negative feedback to which we have alluded in this chapter tend to result in an interesting, yet troubling paradox for managers who want to be open communicators. Specifically, employees often think of their managers as the single most important source of feedback for their work behavior and performance (Ashford, 1986). However, it appears that more feedback is not always better. Instead, there appears to be a growing feedback gap; that is, less feedback or less accurate feedback might be flowing from manager to employee. Given our discussion of how negative feedback can be perceived and reacted to, this might not be too surprising. However, it also is not optimal for individual or organizational performance if accurate feedback is not being communicated.

Moss and Sanchez (2004) attributed the feedback gap to both employees and managers. An employee will engage in feedback avoidance behavior by either avoiding the manager or by diverting the manager's attention to other matters so performance problems pertaining to the employee are not on the manager's radar screen. As an example, we are aware of a manager who believes that the best strategy for dealing with his boss is to simply avoid interaction. Feedback avoidance behavior is likely to occur for at least a few key reasons. First, employees might fear negative feedback because it may be ego threatening. This problem is likely to be most problematic for individuals with a performance–prove goal orientation. Individuals with a performance–prove goal orientation seek favorable feedback, feedback that validates their competencies and avoids negative judgments (VandeWalle, Cron, & Slocum, 2001). Second, followers might avoid any negative feedback as a means of impression and reputation management (Moss & Sanchez, 2004). That is, especially if the feedback was to become public in some manner (e.g., in a meeting), the employee's image or reputation could become tarnished, and he or she could be subject to ridicule or enhanced scrutiny in the future.

The communication gap is not only the result of avoidance behavior on the part of followers; it is also a function of managerial behavior. First, some managers tend to practice active management by exception (Bass & Avolio, 1993). Such managers are not very likely to seek out and acknowledge positive behavior and performance. Instead, they are much more active in finding irregularities, mistakes, and so forth, and when they do, their typical reaction is to judge and communicate their disdain or disappointment in a particularly strident manner. Indeed, these managers are highly prone to the fundamental attribution error, whereby the problems or failures of their employees are attributed to the employees' personal flaws (e.g., laziness or incompetence) rather than aspects of the situation (Heider, 1958). Employees tend to prefer no communication or feedback from these managers. Active management by exception is not an effective form of leadership, and indeed, more positive forms of leadership, including contingent reinforcement and inspirational leadership and encouragement, have been shown to be more effective (Lowe, Kroeck, & Sivasubramaniam, 1996).

Conflict avoidance is a second manner in which some managers contribute to the feedback gap (Moss & Sanchez, 2004). In essence, it represents the opposite of active management by exception in that conflict avoiders are simply uncomfortable giving negative feedback. They might have a nurturing style, thus preferring a supportive role regardless of the situation or the severity of the problem behavior on the part of a follower. There is some evidence that female managers are more likely to delay or even distort negative feedback to make it seem more positive (Benedict & Levine, 1988). Two reasons could account for such behavior on the part of women. First, women are more likely to engage in an interactive style of leadership that is relationship oriented and collaborative (Rosener, 1997). Providing negative feedback to followers might be seen as incongruent with an interactive style. Second, women might learn through experience that negative reactions and anger can result on the part of followers when they (women) attempt to provide corrective feedback or discipline (Atwater, Carey, & Waldman, 2001). As a result, they might think twice about confronting followers with negative feedback in the future. In other words, they learn it might be best to simply play the more nurturing role dictated by societal norms and avoid giving negative feedback.

CONCLUSIONS

In sum, providing negative feedback presents an important dilemma for the manager who seeks to be an open communicator. It is clear from the research that providing negative feedback is likely to lead to negative reactions and outcomes. For this reason, followers have a tendency to avoid putting themselves in situations in which they might receive negative feedback, and managers are likely to avoid providing it. Unfortunately, the upshot is that problematic behavior and performance could remain unchecked. We address this dilemma in a later chapter when we explore the delicate tightrope managers must walk when attempting to openly communicate problems they perceive, while avoiding the negative by-products that can result.

TAKEAWAYS

- Using negative feedback as a means to get an employee's attention or to demonstrate who is in charge will likely have unintended negative effects and is not recommended.

- Individuals with low self-esteem will be more accepting of negative feedback but it will likely not motivate better performance unless the person is assured of his or her ability to change.
- Supervisors need to allow those with high self-esteem to save face by providing some positive feedback before negative.
- Use self-appraisals as part of the performance feedback process to see how self-ratings compare to the manager's ratings. Employees who underrate themselves will be motivated by corrective feedback, whereas those who overrate will not see the corrective feedback as motivational.
- Allow feedback recipients to share their thoughts about the situation.
- Feedback providers should have as much factual and objective information as possible, as impressions are often disputed.
- Punishment used without positive reinforcement to control absenteeism is unlikely to be effective.
- Employees will become desensitized to frequent negative feedback.

3

Feedback Provider and Recipient Characteristics

The purpose of this chapter is to provide a better understanding of the likely outcomes of feedback and other aspects of one-on-one communication in organizations by examining the characteristics of the manager as feedback provider, as well as the follower as feedback recipient. We explain how these characteristics can impact the communication process. We discuss the impact of cultural differences, gender differences, and individual characteristics such as self-esteem and personality.

Our continuing focus in this chapter is the paradox or dilemma managers face with regard to the practice of open communication. As we will see, although there are good reasons for managers to be open communicators, there are also a number of their own personal characteristics, as well as the characteristics of followers, that make the open communication process difficult—and, at times, undesirable. We continue to suggest possibilities for managers seeking to harness the power of open communication.

CULTURE AND ONE-ON-ONE COMMUNICATION IN ORGANIZATIONS

The context for communication in organizations is rapidly becoming culturally diverse for two reasons. First, organizations are rapidly becoming more global in nature, and accordingly, managers must deal with a variety of individuals with cultural backgrounds different from their own. Such individuals can include vendors, customers, subordinates, coworkers, and others. Second, even domestically, organizations have become more culturally diverse. As an example, it is not unusual to hear Spanish spoken in many organizational settings in the United States.

This increasing diversity presents both opportunities and challenges to people in leadership positions who want to effectively communicate. For example, there is evidence that diverse groups make more creative and higher quality decisions and encourage new product and service development (Adler, 1980, 2002). However, cultural diversity also can present challenges to effective interpersonal communication. Western models of managerial behavior do not adequately consider the importance of culture and its influence on individuals' desires and behaviors, especially in Asian-Pacific countries such as Japan and China (Adler, Doktor, & Redding, 1986). As a result, managers are left without guidance about how to effectively communicate with or provide feedback to those in other cultures. In considering the potential effects of culture on manager one-on-one communication, we first consider relevant dimensions of culture identified in the literature.

THE COMMUNICATION IMPLICATIONS OF CULTURE

Hofstede (1980, 2001) and more recently House, Hanges, Javidan, Dorfman, and Gupta (2004) discussed characteristics of cultures that impact the ways in which individuals from different backgrounds perceive the world and the ways in which they communicate and interact with one another. We consider two primary dimensions here, power distance and individualism, common to conceptualizations of culture. First, *power distance* reflects the extent to which members of society accept inequality among those at different hierarchical levels as legitimate. Countries relatively high on power distance, meaning they are more accepting of inequalities, include Mexico, the Philippines, Germany, Nigeria, and India. Countries relatively low on power distance include the United States, Canada, Denmark, and Israel.

Those from low-power-distance countries will expect more two-way communication and the opportunity to discuss issues before decisions are made, whereas those from high-power-distance cultures will be more accepting and less likely to want to challenge decisions. There are many examples in the United States of subordinates becoming upset after a decision is made or announced, not because they disagreed with the decision, but simply because they felt they had insufficient input. This would be far less likely in a culture with high power distance.

A second dimension is individualism versus collectivism. *Individualism* refers to dispositions to understand oneself primarily in terms of one's personal goals and aspirations, whereas *collectivism* refers to the disposition to understand oneself by attending to group needs. Collectivists use group welfare as a principle referent and sacrifice self-interest for the good of the group. Individualists emphasize their own attitudes, values, preferences, and self-interest. As delineated most recently by Gelfand,

Bhawuk, Nishii, and Bechtold (2004), individualism and collectivism can be broken down in terms of levels of analysis. That is, the construct can be conceived at the institutional or societal level, as well as at the in-group or family level. Moreover, it is possible for a culture to vary in terms of its degree of societal versus in-group collectivism. For example, the United States tends to be relatively low on in-group collectivism, although somewhat higher on societal-level collectivism. However, countries such as China, the Philippines, and Singapore are high on both aspects of collectivism.

Because collectivists tend to accept personal blame for failure, negative feedback might be reacted to severely. Managers might need to soften negative feedback when delivering it to individuals from collectivist cultures relative to those from individualist cultures because of the need to save face (Adler, 2002). *Face* is identified as affecting self-respect and dignity, poise, and the ability to maintain a public appearance or self-respect, similar to impression management (Schlenker, 1980). Face has also been described as "one of an individual's most sacred possessions" (Deutsch, 1961, p. 897). As articulated by Goffman (1955), *face work* refers to the subtle style in interpersonal encounters, found in all societies, intent on sidestepping or avoiding public and personal embarrassment. Ironically, this is not to say collectivists do not appreciate or desire negative feedback. In fact, collectivists might actually desire failure feedback because they do not want their failure to negatively impact the group. Receiving negative or failure feedback can ultimately improve the group's welfare.

Because feedback is individually focused in Western cultures and used to further the individual rather than the group, failure feedback is perhaps even more threatening to the individualist. As such, individualists would be expected to avoid failure feedback more than collectivists. In fact, Bailey, Chen, and Dou (1997) found that individuals in Japan and China expressed stronger desires for failure feedback than those in the United States, whereas those in the United States expressed the strongest desires for success feedback.

Although it is not one of Hofstede's (1980, 2001) four cultural dimensions, others studying culture and communication have defined what they refer to as high- and low-context communication cultures (Hall, 1976). In high-context cultures, individuals expect the other involved in the communication to know what that individual has on his or her mind so he or she does not need to be specific. Individuals in high-context cultures tend to talk around the point rather than getting to it directly. In contrast, the dominant North American (low-context) temperament calls for clear and direct communication (e.g., "Don't beat around the bush … get to the point"; Levine, 1985). In most instances, high context and low context are synonymous with collectivist and individualistic, respectively. In high-context (collectivist) cultures, when individuals disagree, the issue is tied closely with the people disagreeing. To disagree openly or confront someone in public is an insult and causes both sides to lose face. Thus, even if the issue is resolved, if one or both parties feel they have lost face, there can be hard feelings between those who disagreed. Alternatively, in low-context cultures, individuals can fight with one another and disagree with loud voices and remain friends afterward. Therefore, two individuals, one from a high-context culture such as India, and one from a low-context culture such as the United States, could have an argument and leave the situation with very different feelings about its outcomes. The Indian could see the situation as a severe threat to the relationship, whereas the American could see it merely as a conflict being resolved.

The Western attribution style for success and failure is a demonstration of the individualistic nature of Western cultures. The self-serving bias, or the tendency to take credit for success and deny blame for failure, is largely a Western or individualistic phenomenon. Americans are typically quick to take credit for their successes. The Japanese tend to demonstrate the opposite attribution style, denying credit for success and taking personal responsibility for failure. Failure attributions in China also are likely to be accepted by individuals as being based on their own undesirable behaviors, such as a lack of effort or perseverance. The Chinese are less likely to take pride in their successes to appear modest (Stipek, Weiner, & Li, 1989). Because one builds a reputation in China largely on the basis of social relationships (Hwang, 1987), attributions are generally made to preserve and to promote group harmony rather than to distinguish oneself as better than others. We recently hired two new Chinese female professors at our university. During our first round of self-assessments as part of the performance appraisal process each of these women rated themselves as unsatisfactory (1 on a 4-point scale) on research. They were new, untenured professors with no publications. Clearly by our standards they were not unsatisfactory, as they needed time to develop a research program and get papers accepted at journals. In contrast, we also hired two native-born western European professors, a woman and a man. These professors also had no publications but rated themselves as outstanding (4 on a 4-point scale). This is a clear demonstration of the influence of culture on self-assessment and modesty.

One of the implications of the phenomenon just described has to do with public praise. Collectivists do not want to be singled out publicly, even for praise. However, individualists are very happy to receive public praise. Additionally, collectivists tend to assume collective blame; that is, the group is to blame for failure. In contrast, individualists spend much time trying to figure out who is responsible for the failure and are rarely willing to assume blame for another. So, if a manager has a policy of announcing his or her subordinates' accomplishments (e.g., announcing when someone has a paper published), some of that manager's subordinates might find this very rewarding whereas others find it embarrassing. Perhaps this manager would do well to ask the subordinates if they mind having their accomplishment announced. Additionally, if the manager comes from a collectivist culture, the manager might not recognize the importance of individual feedback to individualist followers.

Individualism also impacts the extent to which individuals feel free to openly speak their minds. The value orientation of individualism propels North Americans to speak their minds freely through direct verbal expressions. Individualistic values foster the norms of honesty and openness, which are achieved through the use of precise, straightforward language behaviors. The value orientation of collectivism, in contrast, constrains members of cultures such as those in China, Japan, and Korea from speaking boldly through an explicit verbal communication style. Collectivist cultures like China, Japan, and Korea emphasize the importance of group harmony and group conformity: "Group harmony and conformity are accomplished through the use of imprecise, ambiguous verbal communication behaviors" (Gudykunst, Ting-Toomey, & Chua, 1988, p. 102). For example, if a supervisor presents an idea to a culturally mixed group of employees and asks for their reactions, Koreans are much less likely to make definitive statements such as "No, that isn't right," or "I disagree with you." Instead, they are more likely to use such expressions as, "I agree with you in principle," or "I understand your point of view." This indirect approach is used to allow the other individual to save face, which open disagreement would not allow. To a North American, these indirect comments are often taken as support for the idea because Americans presume if they were not supportive, they would have directly said so. The North Americans might not recognize the stylistic difference, and likely, the Korean could have misgivings just like the North American. They have just expressed their misgivings in a different way.

This type of indirect language approach is also evidenced in Japan and other collectivist cultures, where what is said orally might only indirectly represent reality. Those from a collectivist culture are likely to use hints to suggest their beliefs and expect the listener to detect what the speaker really means. It is important in these cultures for the listener to pay attention to nonverbal cues and other indicators to infer what the speaker really feels or means. It is easy to see how this style will cause difficulties with North American speakers who speak their minds and make themselves understood by their words. If nonverbal cues were important, they might be entirely missed.

For example, it is common for the Japanese and those from other Asian countries to nod their heads in the affirmative when listening. This nodding indicates that the listener is paying attention but does not necessarily indicate that the listener agrees with the speaker. To Westerners, nodding in the affirmative indicates agreement. As an example, one of us was recently in a meeting with a colleague from India. The individuals with whom we were having a discussion were presenting a viewpoint completely contrary and in disagreement with our point of view, yet my Indian colleague nodded affirmatively as the group representative spoke. Although it was apparent that this was not an indication of agreement, based on past experience with his nonverbal behaviors, it was worrisome that the individual speaking did not understand the Indian's behavior (i.e., that his nodding was not an indication of his agreement). Those from the other group might have left the encounter believing that they had swayed the Indian gentleman to their viewpoint, which was not at all the case.

Cultural differences, such as nodding not indicating agreement, hesitance to take initiative, failing to admit when one does not understand, and a reluctance to participate in decisions, can represent challenges to managers and employees alike when cultural differences are present in the workplace. The solution to these problems is awareness and sometimes training to deal with such cross-cultural communication issues.

We should note similar direct–indirect styles are evidenced between North Americans and individuals from Arab countries like Egypt. Indirectness in the Arab communication style is demonstrated by a tendency to accommodate, or go along with others. The values of conformity and collectivism lead to smoothing and indirect communication styles, unlike the individualistic, assertive styles of North Americans that lead to direct, to-the-point approaches. One can imagine a discussion between an Egyptian manager and a North American employee not going well if the manager is attempting to accommodate, while the employee is being direct and assertive. Neither will leave the conversation with a good understanding of the other's message.

Another difference between Arab cultures and North American cultures is the propensity for Arab language to use numerous metaphors, similes, and long strings of adjectives. Again, to a direct, straightforward North American, this could be perceived as evasive and an unwillingness to get to the point. It could even be perceived as dishonest or hiding the truth.

There are also differences in expected degrees of formality in conversation. North Americans tend to be very informal, shunning titles, and ritualistic manners with others. For example, when introduced as Dr. Young, or Mrs. Smith, the North American will likely reply, "You can call me Tom," or "Please, call me Cheri." The Japanese, in contrast, prefer formality because such a protocol for them allows for predictable and smooth interactions (Okabe, 1983). For example, there are five different words in Japanese for *you*. The different forms are indicative of the relative rank and status of the speaker and the receiver (Gibson, 1997). The Japanese also take great pride in presenting their business cards and consider it a great insult if someone casually shoves the card in his pocket or her purse. Business cards should be handled with respect and placed on the table carefully in front of the person that receives them. These are minor examples of the ways in which degrees of formality differ across cultures and could impede communication if not understood.

CULTURE AND ITS IMPLICATIONS
FOR FEEDBACK PROCESSES

There are many ways in which cultural differences influence one-on-one communication, especially feedback processes. For example, societies differing in power distance will sanction the same behavior differently. In a society high on power distance, criticism of the manager constitutes a threat to the social order and the hierarchy and will be more strongly condemned than in a society low on power distance. The same criticism delivered by a subordinate to a superior will be less against the prevailing norms and social order in a low-power-distance culture. Thus, criticism from a subordinate to a superior will be reacted to more negatively in a low-power-distance culture.

Power distance is relevant to delivery of negative feedback. In high-power-distance cultures such as Malaysia, criticism from someone of higher status will be more readily accepted, merely because of the person's status. In lower power distance cultures (e.g., the United States or Denmark), the feedback will be considered more for its validity and the source of the feedback will be less relevant. Similarly in low-power-distance countries, subordinates providing corrective feedback upward are more easily accepted than in higher power distance countries. This helps explain why upward feedback as a leadership development tool has not caught on in many Asian and Middle Eastern countries like it has in the United States and much of Europe.

Regarding criticism from manager to follower, Bond, Wan, Leung, and Giacalone (1985) found that Chinese participants were far more accepting of criticism when it came from a high-status individual. In contrast, the status of the feedback provider only modestly influenced the acceptability of criticism on the part of Americans. Injustice and inequality also are better tolerated in high-power-distance cultures but seen as highly unacceptable in low-power-distance cultures (Gudykunst et al., 1988). This suggests that even if the criticism is perceived as inaccurate or unfair, it will be reacted to with more acceptance in high-power-distance cultures.

Let's consider an example of a manager from an Arab country (high power distance) and an employee from the United States (low power distance). If the employee believes the manager is in need of some constructive criticism and decides to provide it, the criticism will likely not be accepted well. Similarly, the Arab manager delivering constructive feedback to the American employee will expect that feedback to be respected and accepted due to their status difference. In fact, the employee might choose to dispute or ignore the feedback. It would be useful for these two individuals from different cultures to realize how their cultural values are impacting their communication styles and expectations.

A recent example occurred when we were conducting multisource feedback for a large computer company. The feedback process was being implemented for senior managers as a development tool. Their subordinates were anonymously surveyed about their leadership competencies, and the data were aggregated and compiled into a confidential report for the manager. There was one relatively new member to the senior management team who was from India. He was initially reluctant to take part in the process, but he ultimately agreed. When we received the survey data from his subordinates, every survey contained the exact same answers, answered with the same ink, and the answers and ink were identical to that in his self-survey. Rather than have subordinates complete the surveys, which would have violated the norms of his high-power-distance culture, he had decided to participate, but to complete the forms himself. Obviously, this was not going to provide him with any useful feedback, but to his colleagues it appeared as though he had participated, even though he was unwilling to ask his subordinates for feedback. As a caveat, we are not trying to imply that all managers from high-power-distance cultures will attempt to use such strategies when they are involved in a multisource feedback process. However, given the cultural background of this manager, such actions should not be surprising.

Stull (1988) provided a good discussion of techniques for giving feedback to foreign-born employees. For example, he suggested the following: (a) simplify, specify, and clarify; (b) allow conversation to go back and forth; and (c) ask for feedback to ensure that your audience is capturing your message. It is also important to choose simple words and try to avoid slang, figures of speech, and sarcasm. Non-Americans do not always understand colloquialisms or when things are said tongue in cheek, and even what tongue in cheek means! Similar lessons apply to subordinates working for a foreign-born manager. Table 3.1 summarizes some feedback lessons for different cultural characteristics.

Case Example

Alex Yang is a Korean manager for Botox, Inc. He is an experienced, competent electrical engineer, recently promoted to a managerial position. Dan Miller reports to Alex. Dan is the team manager for one of the projects Alex supervises. Alex has received a number of complaints from team members on Dan's team. They complain that Dan is loud and overbearing, pushes his ideas too forcefully, refuses to listen to others, and believes he always has the right answer. They are tired of his arrogant manner. Two of the top-notch workers on the team have asked to be reassigned. Alex knows he needs to have a talk with Dan. Given what you've read in this chapter, how would you advise Alex to proceed?

Analysis

Alex is Asian and likely to prefer a subtle, indirect conversation style. He will likely be reluctant to confront Dan. If he does, he will likely try to subtly get Dan to see the problem. Dan has high self-esteem,

TABLE 3.1 Providing Feedback Within Different Cultural Characteristics

Individualist	Collectivist	High Power Distance	Low Power Distance
Provide direct individual feedback	Avoid direct confrontations	Accept criticism from high-status individuals	Criticism of superiors acceptable
Public praise welcome	Avoid public praise or criticism; allow individual to save face		
Expect open disagreement	Expect indirect disagreement	Resist seeking upward feedback	Accepting of upward feedback
Nodding indicates agreement	Nodding indicates attention	Focus on top-down communication	Provide opportunities for two-way communication
Informal	Formal		
Tend to avoid failure feedback	More accepting of failure feedback		

is extroverted, and might even have narcissistic tendencies. Indirect feedback, particularly if it is negative, will likely be ignored. He will blame his lazy team members and be angry that they went to his boss with their complaints. Alex will be amazed his subtle approach with Dan does not have its intended effect.

In this case, Alex will need to leave his comfort zone to confront Dan. He should be armed with as many clear facts as possible, rather than mere perceptions. He will need to confront Dan directly and perhaps more than once. It is also important for Alex to recognize that Dan might see his manager's behavior as very out of character and inconsistent with how he is "expected" to behave. Stereotypically, Asians are not expected to be direct and confrontational. Alex will need to express confidence in Dan that he can turn the situation around and regain the respect of his team members.

Suggestions for Improving Cross-Cultural Communication

Language and cultural differences both contribute to communication barriers across cultures. When trying to communicate with someone who speaks another language, an interpreter will be necessary. Shorter sentences, slowed speech, and simple language will be helpful. It is also important to avoid cultural expressions and colloquial expressions, as these might be taken literally in the other language. "Get off the dime," "Go with the flow," and other such expressions can create confusion when misunderstood. Repeating and summarizing are also helpful. It is important to be patient and recognize that your communication partner is experiencing the same difficulties you are. He or she is having similar frustrations, wondering if his or her message is being clearly communicated. Do not hesitate to ask questions to confirm that your receiver understands, or that you understand the messages being sent.

PERSONALITY AND COMMUNICATION

Personality and individual differences in style and temperament influence the techniques one uses to communicate with others, as well as the way in which feedback is interpreted and reacted to. Among the most studied characteristics relevant to communication are authoritarianism, achievement orientation, pessimism, introversion, and narcissism. We discuss each of these characteristics next.

Authoritarianism

Different socialization practices result in differences in the extent to which people internalize moral values and consider punishment appropriate for wrongdoing (Miller & Vidmar, 1981). Research on the relationship between authoritarianism and punishment has shown those high on authoritarianism are more punitive than those low on authoritarianism (Boehm, 1968; Vidmar, 1974). This could be in part because high authoritarians believe punishment is an effective deterrent to future rule or law violations (Vidmar & Crinklaw, 1974). High authoritarians also are more likely to believe offenders are personally responsible for their actions, whereas low authoritarians stress environmental factors more. High authoritarians are even more likely to ascribe personal responsibility if the offender has low status or is dissimilar to them. We can extrapolate that individuals high on authoritarianism would be more likely to assume personal responsibility for their own wrongdoing if they recognize they have done wrong. They might be more willing to accept punishment or negative feedback because they do assume this responsibility. We could also extrapolate that high authoritarian managers would be more likely to deliver punishment or negative feedback than those low on authoritarianism.

Differences in authoritarianism can be particularly problematic when the supervisor is high on authoritarianism and the subordinate is low on this characteristic. Clearly, the way in which the supervisor will expect the follower to communicate with him or her and the way the supervisor will expect his or her requests to be followed might create difficulties for this subordinate. It will be important for the supervisor to recognize that not everyone has the same beliefs and to express these differences in expectations early in the relationship.

Achievement Orientation

Highly achievement-oriented individuals seek to receive positive feedback, whereas less achievement-oriented individuals tend to avoid negative feedback (Atkinson, 1964). Individuals with a high achievement orientation tend to value competence (Harackiewicz & Manderlink, 1984) and prefer situations providing opportunities to assess their competence, that is, situations that provide feedback (Atkinson, 1974; Spence & Helmreich, 1983). Low achievement-oriented individuals do not value competence as much and try to avoid feedback, as they fear the feedback might make them tense about their task performance. As such, low achievement-oriented individuals tend to respond negatively to competence feedback and would prefer not to receive any feedback.

Achievement orientation also influences reactions to positive and negative feedback. Those with high achievement orientation tend to have more severe negative reactions to negative feedback about their competence and more extreme positive reactions to positive feedback about their competence than do those with low achievement orientation. That is, those with low achievement orientation are not as likely to be affected by the feedback. This suggests that negative feedback to individuals with high achievement orientation will reduce their feelings of competence or their ability to do a job or task; thus, their motivation will be reduced as well. However, positive feedback to those with high achievement orientation could be very motivational for future performance. It is critical for managers to recognize that those with high achievement orientation are similar to those with low self-efficacy in terms of their need for positive feedback. Negative feedback needs to be delivered in a way that does not diminish their feelings of competence.

Pessimism

Pessimists and depressives (dysphorics) attend to negative feedback, wanting to know how many people did better than them, whereas optimists (nondysphorics) attend to positive feedback, or want to know how many people did worse than them (McFarland & Miller, 1994). Positively oriented people generally do not attend to negative information and thus react with more anxiety when forced to attend to it than negatively oriented people. Optimists also are more likely to engage in self-enhancement bias than pessimists (Alloy & Ahrens, 1987; Brown, 1986).

Optimists tend to avoid negative feedback because it interferes with their positive view of the world. They might be more likely to discount the feedback because to acknowledge it causes anxiety. The optimists, similar to those with high self-efficacy, will need extra attention from the supervisor to ensure negative feedback is taken seriously.

Introversion

Introverts and anxious persons tend to be more reactive to negative feedback or negative information than extroverts and are more likely to attend to negative cues or signals (Boddy, Carver, & Rowley, 1986; Derryberry, 1987). In addition, introverts are more likely to actually respond to punishment by refraining from the punished behavior in the future (Patterson, Kosson, & Newman, 1987; Pearce-McCall & Newman, 1986). Extroverts are less likely to alter goal-oriented behavior in the face of punishment than introverts. Tiggemann, Winefield, and Brebner (1982) provided evidence that the goal-oriented behavior of extroverts is relatively unsusceptible to the inhibiting effects of punishment. Extroverts do not pause after being punished and cannot process adequately the effects of their maladaptive behavior. Extroverts are "geared to respond" and respond more slowly following negative feedback than introverts (Pearce-McCall & Newman, 1986). This suggests extroverts might need to hear negative feedback more than once to really attend to the feedback and alter behavior.

Narcissism

Narcissistic individuals are characterized by extreme self-centeredness and self-absorption and an excessive need for attention. Not surprisingly, narcissists tend to react very negatively to negative feedback. In a study by Kernis and Sun (1994), although narcissists did not find negative feedback less accurate, they showed more scorn for the person who delivered it. Following negative feedback, narcissism was related to perceiving the evaluator as less competent and likeable. This is consistent with earlier findings that narcissists tend to show more hostility toward the providers of negative feedback because they perceive the providers of negative feedback unfavorably (Kernis & Sun, 1994). Narcissists tend to overreact to negative feedback. This is a case where extra care should be taken in deciding whether it is worth it to deliver the feedback. Perhaps another approach should be taken with the narcissist to get the point across, such as showing him or her how someone else approached a task, without explicitly criticizing the narcissist. Table 3.2 summarizes the lessons on personality and individual characteristics and communication.

GENDER AND ONE-ON-ONE COMMUNICATION

Demographic similarities and differences between feedback recipient and providers have been the subject of much research. Generally, the

TABLE 3.2 Providing Feedback Based on Personality and Individual Characteristics

High Authoritarian	High Achievement Orientation	Low Achievement Orientation	Introverts	Extroverts	Narcissists	Optimists
Believe in value of punishment	Seek positive feedback	Tend to avoid feedback	Attentive to negative feedback	Inattentive to negative feedback	React strongly and negatively to negative feedback	Tend to avoid negative feedback; react with anxiety to negative feedback
Assume responsibility for wrong-doing; more willing to accept negative feedback and punishment	Overreact to negative feedback; must be handled gently	Not very reactive to feedback (positive or negative)		Might need to hear corrective feedback more than once to attend to it	Approach feedback giving cautiously	Tend to overrate themselves
	Positive feedback motivational					

literature suggests that demographic similarity should result in more effective communication because the sender and receiver will be more likely to have similar frames of reference, will identify more closely with one another, and generally will be more responsive to one another (Polzer, Milton, & Swann, 2002).

Gender appears to represent a key variable relevant to demographic fit. A wide variety of research is relevant to understanding gender as a demographic fit variable in relation to one-on-one communication in organizations. For example, Chung, Marshall, and Gordon (2001) found that male subjects gave less positive feedback to hypothetical female supervisees than to male supervisees exhibiting the same performance. Geddes and Konrad (2003) found that men reacted more unfavorably to negative feedback when it was delivered by a woman. However, it is not always the case that demographic differences contribute to communication gaps. Women might not react more negatively to male managers, as opposed to female managers, delivering negative feedback (Geddes & Konrad, 2003), and women might not give less positive feedback to hypothetical men than to women when their performance is the same (Chung et al., 2001).

Stereotypes and Expectations

It appears that stereotypes and expectations might be impacting the extent to which gender differences influence communication. Heilman's (1983) lack of fit model suggests that expectations about how successful an individual will be in a job are influenced by the fit between the perceptions of the individual's attributes and the perceptions of the job requirements. Most traits associated with management are generally considered to be masculine (Brenner, Tomkiewicz, & Schein, 1989). According to the lack of fit model, the skills and abilities perceived to be required to effectively handle masculine sex-typed jobs, such as managerial ones, do not correspond to the attributes believed to characterize women as a group. Taking a leadership role and providing discipline or negative feedback simply are not activities consistent with a view of women as the gentle and relatively passive gender (Heilman, 1983). For example, in the Atwater, Brett, Waldman, DiMare, and Hayden (2003) study, 85% of respondents, when asked whether discipline was a male or female role, indicated providing discipline was a male role.

Eagly and Karau (2002) extended the conceptualization about gender and fit in their presentation of the role incongruity theory of prejudice toward female managers. This theory contends women suffer prejudice when they assume leadership roles because the roles of women and the roles of leaders conflict in many cases. Women are expected to be communal (e.g., kind, nurturing, sensitive, and helpful). Leaders are supposed to be assertive, confident, ambitious, and dominant. Clearly the expectations of leaders are more closely aligned with stereotypical male traits than female traits. That is, women experience a lack of fit between their leadership roles and their female roles. As such, when women must enact many of the leadership roles they are required to enact, such as giving negative feedback, they must balance others' expectations of women with the expectations they have of leaders. Men have no such balancing act to manage.

The feedback issue between male and female managers and followers becomes particularly problematic when women are in leadership positions and men are their subordinates. Men see management as more traditionally male-oriented in nature than do women, and accordingly, men are more likely to react unfavorably toward female bosses than women (Atwater, Carey, & Waldman, 2001; Stevens & DeNisi, 1980). This tendency for difficulties to arise when women supervise men stems in part from what Gutek and Cohen (1987) termed *sex-role spillover*. Essentially, sex-role spillover contends that expected roles for men and women in their social interactions spill over into the workplace. That is, because women are expected to be more submissive, and men more dominant socially, these roles will also be expected in the workplace. As such, when men must report to women, the reporting relationship has additional strains because it violates expected male–female interaction patterns.

There might be a tendency for a woman delivering negative feedback to be reacted to more negatively than a man providing the same feedback. Research has shown that women are devalued when they employ stereo-typically male leadership styles (e.g., nonparticipative; Eagly, Makhijani, & Klonsky, 1992). Additionally, the communication literature supports the notion that when women behave assertively they are rated more negatively than men, particularly when they are engaging in negative assertive behavior, such as giving negative feedback to a subordinate (Rakos, 1991; Wilson & Gallois, 1993). One of the interviewees in the Atwater, Carey, and Waldman (2001) study of discipline commented:

> I think gender had a big part of it simply because she was female. I think she saw me with my stature and stuff and my physical appearance. She thought that this (the discipline) would give her an upper hand to show that she was the dominant person ... she always seemed somewhat intimi-dated by males and I think this was a good deal of it. She relied on the males as far as the technical side so she had to take that attitude.

Another interesting finding from that discipline study was that when women and men delivered discipline, recipients had differing levels of acceptance of responsibility for their behavior. When women delivered discipline to men, the recipient did not accept responsibility for his behavior 45% of the time. When a woman disciplined a woman, the recipient did not accept responsibility for her behavior 52% of the time. However, when a man delivered the discipline, the male and female recipients were unwilling to accept responsibility 37% and 18% of the time, respectively. Particularly interesting here regarding gender roles is the willingness of female recipients to accept responsibility (88% of the time) when the discipline was delivered by a man.

Implications

So what are the implications of gender role fit between managers and subordinates for providing feedback? First, and foremost, we wish to again emphasize that the value of open and direct communication might need to be balanced. In this case, the balance hinges on concerns regarding gender role conflicts. Thus, female managers might need to recognize the potential for subordinates to hold negative biases toward them when they assume male roles such as providing discipline or negative feedback. Women should realize the need to balance their gender roles and leadership roles. There are a number of ways they might do this. For example, female managers might need to provide feedback assertively, yet in a more nurturing or sensitive way than male managers. That is, they need to integrate some of the expected characteristics of both roles in a given situation. It might also be more important for women to show a caring attitude or in some way legitimize the negative feedback. For example, Brett, Atwater, and Waldman (2005) found that when delivering corrective feedback, positive outcomes were more likely to result for female managers when they allowed recipients to express their views and when they provided the feedback in a considerate way. These behaviors did not impact the effectiveness of the feedback when delivered by male managers.

Male and female followers should recognize the tendency they might have to apply inaccurate or distorted perceptions of a female manager's abilities, merely based on their gender expectations and without consideration of the female manager's true abilities. It would also be helpful if followers could recognize the difficult balancing act female managers face and give them a little leeway.

Some research suggests that women are sensitive to the need to modify their feedback delivery styles. For example, there are indications from the communication literature that male and female managers might be likely to use different approaches to providing feedback, and might consider different approaches to be more effective. For example, in attempts to resolve conflicts, female managers are more likely to report that they attempt to use soft tactics and affiliative or personal approaches in their first attempts, whereas men report a higher likelihood to use hard tactics, such as pressure or confrontation (Carothers & Allen, 1999; Pruitt, 1998). Women also report that they are more likely to use soft or affiliative approaches to negotiation (Sagrestano, 1992). These results are compatible with those of Eagly and Johnson's (1990) meta-analysis, in which they found that women were more participative and democratic in their leadership styles than men. Men tended to be more autocratic and directive.

Additional Roles and Questions

There are other managerial roles considered primarily masculine, such as problem solving, strategic decision making, and allocating resources (Atwater et al., 2003). Women will need to be sensitive to the conflicts between their gender expectations and their behavior when engaging in these roles.

A particularly intriguing issue is the extent to which role incongruity issues mentioned here might interact with aspects of culture. For example, are the effects of gender–role incongruity especially problematic in cultures lacking gender egalitarianism? In line with Emrich, Denmark, and Den Hartog (2004), we define gender egalitarianism in terms of the extent to which people in a society believe biological sex determines the nature of the roles individuals should play in society. Societies that seek to minimize differences between the roles of men and women at both home and in other settings (e.g., work settings) can be considered to be gender egalitarian. For example, societies relatively high on gender egalitarianism include Russia, Denmark, Sweden, and Canada. Countries moderate on gender egalitarianism include the United States, Thailand, and Brazil. Countries low on gender egalitarianism include South Korea, Mexico, and Middle Eastern countries such as Kuwait, Egypt, and Morocco (Emrich et al., 2004; Friedrich, Mesquita, & Hatum, 2005). We could expect the role incongruity issue, and its potential negative effects on communication, to be most accentuated in the countries that are lower on gender egalitarianism.

CONCLUSIONS

In sum, we can see the dilemmas managers face when deciding when, how, and how much feedback to provide to followers. A number of individual and cultural characteristics must be considered, as well as the interaction of these characteristics when the manager and follower differ.

TAKEAWAYS

- Individuals from low-power-distance cultures such as the United States expect more two-way communication before decisions are made.
- Managers might need to soften negative feedback when delivering it to individuals from a collectivist culture relative to those from individualist cultures because of the need to save face.
- Be aware that individualists would be expected to avoid failure feedback more than collectivists.
- Those from collectivist cultures do not want to be singled out publicly even for praise. Individualists are very happy to receive public praise.

- Managers would do well to ask subordinates if they mind having their accomplishments announced.
- If the manager comes from a collectivist culture, it is important for the manager to recognize the importance of individual feedback to individualist followers.
- Recognize that collectivists will be less likely to speak directly than individualists.
- It is important for managers to pay attention to nonverbal cues and other indicators when the speaker is from a collectivist culture.
- In a society high on power distance, criticism of the manager constitutes a threat to the social order and the hierarchy and will be more strongly condemned than in a society low on power distance.
- North Americans have very informal communication patterns that are not found in Asian cultures.
- Upward feedback as a leadership development tool will be more readily accepted in the United States and Europe than in Asia or the Middle East.
- When giving feedback to foreign-born employees (a) simplify, specify, and clarify; (b) allow conversation to go back and forth; and (c) ask for feedback to ensure that your audience is capturing your message. It is also important to choose simple words and try to avoid slang, figures of speech, and sarcasm.
- Individuals with a high achievement orientation tend to value competence and prefer situations providing opportunities to assess their competence (i.e., situations that provide feedback). Low achievement-oriented individuals tend to respond negatively to competence feedback and would prefer not to receive feedback.
- Extroverts might need to hear negative feedback more than once to really attend to the feedback and alter behavior.
- Female managers might need to provide feedback assertively, yet in a more nurturing or sensitive way than male managers.
- Negative feedback delivered by female managers to men from cultures low on gender egalitarianism (e.g., Mexico, or the Middle East) will be resisted.

4

Manager as Feedback Recipient

Upward Communication

Upward communication is the means by which information is sent up the chain of command. Upward communication involves communicating the following from below: employee achievements, progress, and plans; unresolved work problems with which employees might need help; feedback to the supervisor about his or her behavior; suggestions and ideas for improvement; and employees feelings about their jobs, associates, and the organization (Rue & Byars, 1995). Upward communication is one of the more important communication channels. It is important for managers and followers, as well as for optimal organizational functioning. The "subordinate-to-superior network is extremely important for organizational health, and it is an aspect of communication that however difficult, must be dealt with to improve the functioning of the organization" (Zaremba, 1993, p. 44). Employees, as well as lower level managers, have important perspectives on organizational issues, valuable expertise, and valuable feedback for managers about ways in which they can improve their management style and effectiveness. Feedback can also act as an early warning system about potential problems and grievances. Kassing and Armstrong (2002), for example, found that individuals with concerns regarding unethical conduct or issues that could result in potential harm will seek the attention of the media or regulatory bodies if supervisors or organizational officials fail to acknowledge their issues.

Clearly, upward communication in organizations is important and managers generally recognize this. Baron (1996) reported that managers believed upward feedback (both positive and negative) was more useful than did subordinates. However, Baron found that managers thought they were doing a better job of encouraging informal upward feedback than their subordinates did. Subordinates did not realize the extent to which managers saw feedback from subordinates as mostly negative.

The ways in which upward communication is delivered and perceived are not entirely agreed on and the effectiveness of upward communication can be improved. Among the factors affecting the effectiveness and openness of upward communication in organizations are characteristics of the organization's culture; employee characteristics, attitudes, and beliefs; characteristics of the managers to whom employees report; and mechanisms in place to provide opportunities for upward communication. We also discuss barriers to upward communication and ways to overcome them in this chapter.

ORGANIZATION CULTURE

The way in which upward communication works in an organization is affected by the fit of the communication with the organization's culture. Organizations with strict hierarchical structures, such as the military and police organizations, will see greater resistance to upward feedback by employees and managers. The first author did an interview with a Navy admiral during a study of military leadership in the 1980s. This gentleman told her that subordinates did not know anything about leadership; you had to be a leader to understand leadership. She recalls thinking it was odd the recipients of leadership would be clueless as to what made for good leadership. Years later, she was doing a study of leadership at the U.S. Naval Academy. She had surveyed underclassmen about the leadership of upperclassmen. The officer in charge suggested the upperclassmen could benefit from learning how their leadership was rated or perceived by their reports. There was much resistance to this idea at the time, but she did as the officer suggested and provided this feedback to the upperclassmen about how they were viewed by their reports. (This was long before multisource feedback had become the rage.) As one might expect, there were many surprised upperclassmen, particularly those who were shocked at their low leadership ratings. Prior to this study, the only information an upperclassman got about his or her leadership came from the company officer (i.e., downward feedback). This feedback often reflected more about the student's followership rather than his or her actual leadership. There were many who believed downward feedback was how it should be and less than positive upward feedback was disrespectful and disruptive to the chain of command. However, the students who received the upward feedback were enlightened and the practice was continued for some time. Over the last 25 years, upward feedback in military organizations has been viewed much more positively and implemented in many places.

In the 1990s, we implemented an upward feedback survey and report process in a police organization. Although this process had become popular in the business world, it was a novelty in police organizations. In fact, at the time, we were not aware of any police organization in the country doing anything like this. Similar to the Navy, there were concerns about the process disrupting the chain of command. Although we met with some resistance when we implemented the process, the organization eventually embraced it and continued the process for 3 years until a new manager, with new ideas, came in to run the department.

Contrast this with the school districts we have been working with recently. The administration of the schools thinks multisource feedback is fantastic, and clearly in line with their organizational culture, which values learning, employee development, and open communication.

The major obstacle we have confronted when implementing upward feedback in business organizations is also reflective of organizational culture. However, in business organizations the primary concern is accountability. Top managers are skeptical about providing confidential feedback to managers. They want to see the ratings the managers get so they can take action on those getting low ratings. Their attitude is that confidential, developmental feedback is not sufficient to motivate change when someone is not a good manager. They want accountability and believe that there need to be carrots and sticks associated with change. Generally, we have been able to convince these managers to keep the feedback confidential, but to require each recipient to write a development plan he or she shares with his or her supervisor. At least this quasi-accountability alleviates some of the anxiety.

As another example, in the police organization discussed earlier, the director of the agency was one of the recipients of upward feedback. The first author met with him one on one to discuss his feedback report. He was very open to the suggestions his reports had provided, but had additional questions about what some of the ratings and comments specifically meant. She suggested he meet with his direct reports as a group to flesh out some of the questions he had. Although he was receptive to this idea, he was very skeptical that his employees would be open and honest to his face. Instead, we held a meeting where the director introduced the issues he had questions about and the first author facilitated the discussion with his subordinates after he left the room. After a lengthy discussion, he rejoined the group and the issues were discussed without attribution to any particular individual. In other, less hierarchical organizations, this approach might not be necessary. The point here is that it is not merely the players, but also the "field" that impacts how upward feedback is perceived (e.g., its value and appropriateness), as well as how or whether it is delivered.

EMPLOYEE CHARACTERISTICS

Probably the most relevant employee attitude affecting upward communication is fear of retaliation. "Workers generally will not speak their minds if they know their comments will reach management with their names attached" (Ettorre, 1997, p. 1). There is a presumption, often accurate, on the employee's part that if he or she brings bad news or complaints he or she will be seen as "not a team player," a troublemaker, or someone who would be better off working elsewhere. As such, many problems go unreported and unresolved, and talented but dissatisfied employees leave the organization. There is a variety of things that can be done to help alleviate this reluctance, including demonstrating the messenger will not be "killed," providing anonymity, and open-door policies.

HOW TO HELP EMPLOYEES EFFECTIVELY COMMUNICATE UPWARDLY

Employees must know how to make good decisions about what to communicate. No manager wants to see the same employee in his or her office every other day with another complaint or suggestion. However, neither does the manager want good ideas to go unnoticed or complaints to get out of hand. Thus, employees must know how to effectively communicate upward (Green & Knippen, 1999). For example, the employee should attempt to identify specific actions the manager does to make it hard for him or her to communicate with the manager (e.g., unavailability, defensiveness, and disinterest). Once identified, the employee needs to decide what can be done to alleviate the problem. Perhaps instead of dropping by the manager's office 10 times only to find him or her at a meeting, the employee could make an appointment to see the manager. It is also important when doing so to give the manager an indication of the subject of the discussion (e.g., conflict with a co-worker, suggestion for improvement, etc.).

Employees also should try to identify the reasons for their own reluctance to communicate with the manager (e.g., conflict avoidant, shy, do not think it will matter or they will be listened to). Again, how can these issues be addressed? Perhaps the employee could role-play with a coworker before addressing the manager to get feedback about his or her approach.

One example of how upward feedback can be used advantageously in organizations is for the employee to communicate to a manager what he or she finds motivating or demotivating.

Case Example

A relatively new employee goes into the boss's office to ask for a signature on a proposal that requires the boss's signature. Writing proposals was a valued activity and one the boss had encouraged. The new employee presents the boss with the proposal and signature page, expecting him to provide positive recognition for the employee's efforts. Instead the boss merely says, "I hope if this proposal gets approved it isn't going to cost this department anything because if it will, I'm not going to sign this." The employee assures the boss that there will be no costs to the department. The boss signs the signature page. Rather than leaving feeling good about her accomplishment, however, the employee leaves disappointed and angry because the boss provided no recognition of her hard work on the proposal. Rather than harboring negative feelings toward the boss, the employee returns to her office and calls the boss on the phone, indicating she needs to talk to him. He says, "I'll come down to your office." The employee then explains her disappointment and suggests it would be helpful to motivate her if he could try to be more encouraging and positive in the future. Actually, this feedback helps and the boss does try to provide positive recognition to the employee in the future when it is warranted.

Analysis

In this case the employee effectively communicated her preferred supervisory style and the result was positive. The manager tried to accommodate her by providing more positive reinforcement in the future.

There are a number of factors that make it more or less likely employees will provide upward feedback. Employees are more likely to exercise voice upward when (a) they are satisfied with their jobs and their supervisors, (b) they are more invested in their jobs, (c) they perceive long-term employment security, and (d) they feel loyal to the organization (cf. Ferrell & Rusbult, 1992). Alternatively, they are less likely to provide upward feedback when they are cynical about the organization.

Research over the past 10 to 15 years indicates that cynicism is on the rise in U.S. business and industry. Cynicism hurts business and impedes change. Cynics believe "the best way to handle people is to tell them what they want to hear," "it doesn't pay to work hard," "managers rarely reveal the real reasons behind decisions," and "people are just out for themselves" (Mirvis & Kanter, 1991). Mirvis and Kanter (1991) described cynical companies as those embodying expedient, self-serving values; that support managers who engage in deceptive and exploitative practices; and communicate in a one-sided, hyped-up, and disingenuous fashion to their employees. The aspects of company life that most often disillusion people and promote cynicism are perceptions of an unfair pay or reward system and feelings that management cannot be trusted or the company does not care. It is easy to see how organizational cynicism can be deadly to open and honest communication between managers and employees. Cynicism can lead to generalized mistrust of anyone in a position of authority; bad-mouthing of management, their messages, and directives; and overall vilification of the leadership in an organization.

The effects of organizational cynicism on the part of managers receiving multisource feedback have also been investigated. Managers who were more cynical about the organization (e.g., believe change is unlikely, have given up trying to improve things, believe people in the organization have bad attitudes) were less likely to respond positively, or make positive changes, in response to feedback from subordinates (Atwater, Waldman, Atwater, & Cartier, 2000).

However, cynicism is not a given. Managers can take steps to minimize or reduce cynical attitudes on the part of employees. First, genuine, honest communication is essential. The rationale for decisions must be accurately and widely communicated. "Embargoed" information should only be used when absolutely necessary. In our experience, trying to keep information from employees until it is right for them to know often backfires. All it takes is a few of these embargoed communications to leak out early, which they usually will no matter what prevention methods are used, and management will not be trusted for years.

Second, managers must work particularly hard to design and implement a fair pay and reward system. It is important for employees to believe their voices are heard and it is also important to see managers operating in an above-board, honest manner. We have all seen cases where rewards or pay raises were given for reasons other than good performance, sometimes even to keep a disgruntled employee quiet. These types of decisions will perpetuate cynicism and negative attitudes and reduce upward communication.

Cynicism can be modified but it takes time and repeated demonstrations where employees see managers actually taking steps to implement their ideas.

MANAGER CHARACTERISTICS AND BEHAVIORS

A manager's personality and behavior toward employees attempting to deliver upward communication can influence the extent to which upward communication occurs and can increase or decrease the communication gap.

Consider the following scenario. A new manager arrives on the job and in his first staff meeting with his employees he touts the value of upward communication and his openness toward it. A few weeks later, one of the manager's employees stops by his office to share some feedback. It seems a number of employees are upset because the manager is rarely in his office, and no one knows how to get in touch with him when a problem arises. The manager proceeds to deny the accusations and becomes very defensive with the employee. The manager subsequently berates the employee to others, calling him needy and a whiner. Guess how much upward feedback this manager will get in the future?

Alternatively, suppose the same upward feedback is provided to a different manager. That manager then thanks the employee for the feedback, purchases a cell phone, and publicizes the number to all employees, indicating his interest in being available when needed. Now the word gets back that the manager truly meant what he said and open communication is truly valued.

Certain manager personality traits also make them more or less likely to be open to upward communication. For example, older managers tend to seek less feedback and also tend to have less accurate self-perceptions (more inflated) than younger, less experienced managers. Managers who feel insecure or who have low self-esteem also could be expected to be less receptive to upward communication, particularly if the communication is in any way critical of the manager. Employees should recognize these possibilities and work harder, although carefully, at getting their voices heard.

Other inhibitors of upward communication include managers who do not listen. We all have experience with managers who appear to be listening, but we can hear them typing on their computer while they listen to us on the phone, or they are checking their Blackberry while we talk. These are clear signs active listening is not taking place. However, managers also can appear to be listening, yet the minute the subordinate leaves the room the manager has totally forgotten his or her issue or what the manager said she would do. It is very important to encourage upward communication with active listening and follow-up. Managers need to let subordinates know that they have looked into employee concerns and the results of those efforts.

Managers who get defensive and argue with the feedback being provided are more likely to inhibit future upward communication attempts. At a minimum the manager needs to acknowledge the subordinate's perspective or opinion even if he or she does not agree with it.

Managers who penalize for candor, or "shoot the messenger," also discourage open communication. We have certainly seen organizations where no one wants to tell the emperor he has no clothes for fear of reprisal. This reprisal could take the form of public criticism or withdrawing of support for the messenger's initiatives. The resulting reluctance on the part of subordinates to be honest leads to ineffective decisions on the part of managers who are operating with incomplete information.

MECHANISMS TO PROMOTE UPWARD COMMUNICATION

Suggestion Boxes

One mechanism used by many companies is anonymous suggestion boxes. These allow employees to provide upward feedback without fear of retaliation if managers are unhappy with the comments. However, allowing employees to say anything with no accountability has its drawbacks and the feedback can be unpleasant for managers to hear or take seriously. Although anonymity and suggestion boxes serve a purpose, Housel and Davis (1977) found employees were more likely to use an upward communication channel if they could do it face to face rather than in writing, due to the permanence of record. Managers also were more satisfied with upward communication when it could be delivered face to face.

Focus groups or exit interviews conducted by outsiders, those with no involvement with the organization (e.g., outside consultants), also can be a valuable means for collecting honest, upward communication.

Open-Door Policies

Some managers adopt what they refer to as open-door policies. In essence, this means anyone from any level in the organization can have direct access to upper level managers. Often, managers will set a time each week when they will be available for individuals to walk in and discuss issues on their minds. Others allow employees to set up appointments for open discussion. However, the ways in which these open-door policies actually work vary. In one organization the first author worked in, the manager who truly had an open-door policy was replaced by one who claimed to have an open-door policy, but his behavior suggested otherwise. Manager 1 (Don) had his desk facing the door so he could see anyone who walked in. He had a chair in front of his desk where he invited visitors to sit. When you spoke he gave you his undivided attention. Manager 2 (Pete) had his desk facing an interior wall. When you came to his door he would say "Come in," but would not even look around or make eye contact. He would ask you what you wanted and never even look up from his computer. Don obviously encouraged more upward communication than Pete, yet they both claimed to have an open-door policy. Others claim to have an open door, yet immediately ask if you have consulted with a lower level manager. Obviously some issues should be taken up with one's direct supervisor, but a true open-door manager would listen and then refer.

Multisource Feedback

Multisource or 360-degree feedback has become a popular technique for obtaining upward feedback about an individual manager's behavior or performance. Multisource feedback is a process where a manager's boss, peers, subordinates, and sometimes customers are asked to provide feedback via survey about the manager's behavior or performance in a number of areas. For all but the boss, this feedback is anonymous and most often it is confidential and used strictly for development of the manager; it is not shared with others for evaluative purposes.

A great deal has been written about multisource feedback and recommendations for its implementation (see, e.g., Bracken, Timmreck, & Church, 2001). In this chapter we focus on the factors encouraging honest responses and ways in which managers can use the feedback to their best advantage.

If raters believe feedback to the managers will be for the managers' use only, they are more likely to respond honestly, and less leniently, than if they believe it will be used for evaluative decisions (London, 2001). This suggests that when managers attempt to collect multisource feedback for evaluative decisions, the feedback the manager receives might not be as honest or useful as one might hope. Also, managers feel less need to be defensive and to discount the validity of the ratings if they are provided confidentially. As mentioned earlier in the chapter, top managers worry that if feedback is not shared with their supervisor, there is no accountability for change. This might be true; when supervisors get to see a subordinate manager's feedback they can make more informed decisions about the manager's performance. Yet, more accountability might not always be a good thing, as it can create game playing with high rating exchanges, or encourage managers to be overly lenient with subordinates to receive high ratings from them. In a work setting it might cause a manager to go too easy on subordinates to get good ratings, and the ultimate result is lower performance. One possibility is to assess measurable, objective outcomes (e.g., budget, productivity) for evaluative decisions, and ratings of manager behaviors for development (Bracken, 1996).

Open-ended comments are also a useful component of 360-degree evaluations and most helpful when raters are encouraged to provide problems and solutions (London, 2003). However, in a study done by Rose and Farrell (2002), of the 1,324 comments they reviewed, only 25% included both problem and solution. It is advisable to encourage raters to be constructive and helpful rather than merely providing criticism. Caution is also encouraged when using open-ended comments, as some subordinates might see this as an opportunity to say things that they would never say to the manager face to face. These comments can, at times, even be embarrassing. In three cases we are aware of, feedback recipients were stunned by their raters' candor. In one case the manager was encouraged to spend fewer hours on the golf course. In a second case comments were about poor hygiene. In a third case the feedback to the manager was to cut back on her alcohol consumption and to spend more time with her kids. Although these might have all been prudent suggestions, in every case the manager was visibly embarrassed.

With respect to providing the manager with upward feedback about his or her strengths, the majority of the comments regarding strengths were not useful for development. They are, however, useful for helping diminish negative reactions to the feedback, and even negative reactions to embarrassing comments.

Another way to improve upward communication is to ask managers to meet with their rater groups following feedback. Walker and Smither (1999) found managers who discussed their feedback with raters made more improvements as measured by subsequent ratings. They might have gotten additional helpful feedback that helped them improve, or perhaps their raters believed they were trying harder and gave them higher ratings the second time around. As provided in the earlier example about the police director, the additional feedback gleaned from a group meeting can be very useful.

When the first author worked as a department chair, she requested upward feedback from the faculty and staff in her department. They completed anonymous surveys that were aggregated into a report for her. After she reviewed the report, she met with the staff and faculty as separate groups. She put the strengths and weaknesses the groups had identified up on flip charts and asked a faculty member to get additional feedback from the group, particularly about areas in need of improvement. This candid feedback was very helpful in providing a better understanding of her development needs. For example, the scores she received on "available when needed" were lower than she expected. She was surprised by this because she made a point to be in her office every day and everyone had her home phone number. As a result of the group meeting, she learned being available did not mean that she was not physically available, but she always seemed so busy her subordinates did not want to bother her. Clearly, this was something she needed to work on!

Ilgen and Davis (2000) suggested the way feedback is framed or presented might influence how recipients react emotionally and cognitively to the feedback. Delivering negative feedback is particularly challenging, as recipients tend to react with anger and discouragement rather than with motivation to improve (Brett & Atwater, 2001). It is important that feedback be presented in a way that focuses the individuals' attention on their behavior, or performance, rather than on themselves and their self-worth, or their performance relative to others. Attention to self produces emotional reactions more likely to interfere with performance and to deplete the cognitive and motivational resources the individual needs for task performance (Kanfer & Ackerman, 1989). In this vein, Atwater and Brett (in press) provided 360-degree feedback to recipients in one of two formats: traditional 360-degree feedback format, which includes multi-source averaged ratings as well as normative group comparisons, or text feedback without numeric scores, only text that indicated a particular behavior was a strength or a development need. They hypothesized that the text feedback would be reacted to more positively than the numeric scores because the text would be less threatening to the recipient's self-concept and would cause less focus on self. This hypothesis was not supported. Rather Atwater and Brett found individuals reacted more positively to scores and normative data. They thought the text feedback was vague and they preferred seeing the actual scores they had received on the items. That is, they reported more positive emotions, fewer negative emotions (anger and discouragement), and more motivation to improve when they received numeric ratings.

Atwater and Brett (2005) also found recipients' immediate reactions to feedback (30 minutes after they received their feedback report) predicted positive and negative change in the number of strengths and development needs identified by their raters a year later. Unfortunately, however, the pattern was not what we would like. In essence, individuals who received feedback with many development needs reacted with more anger and discouragement and less motivation to improve. These individuals had more development needs 1 year later (controlling for their Time 1 feedback). Those who got positive feedback were more motivated and had fewer development needs 1 year following feedback. This further reinforces the importance of providing negative feedback in a constructive, supportive manner (perhaps using coaches) to attempt to minimize negative immediate reactions to the feedback.

Coaches

Smither, London, Flautt, Vargas, and Kucine (2002) found that executives who worked with a coach following multisource feedback improved more than those who did not work with a coach. This supports the suggestion made by Brett and Atwater (2001) that individuals who receive negative feedback might need follow-up sessions with a facilitator or an executive coach to help them deal constructively with the results. Some of the coaching steps as outlined by Smither and Reilly (2001) follow. The coach should:

1. Establish rapport with the manager. The manager should feel comfortable being frank with the coach and should trust that the coach has his or her best interests at heart.
2. Identify the manager's performance development needs. This will likely be based in part on the feedback report the manager received, and embellished perhaps by discussions with the manager and other rater groups.
3. Work with the manager to set specific goals and development plans.
4. Identify what actions the manager needs to take to achieve the goals and plans.
5. Evaluate progress toward goals and discuss progress with the manager. Then reassess and set new goals as needed.

UPWARD COMMUNICATION REGARDING PERFORMANCE APPRAISALS

Studies show that most managers get little or no training in how to conduct performance appraisals. The 25% who do get training usually only learn now to deal with the administrative aspects, such as how to fill out forms, when they are due, and so on (Swan & Margulies, 1991), so many managers might be poorly prepared to conduct performance appraisals. However, these appraisals are used to make many decisions important to the employee and the organization. For example, a survey of more than 500 organizations revealed that 87% of managers use performance appraisals in making compensation decisions, 45% use them to make promotion decisions, and over 30% use them to make retention and discharge decisions. Not surprisingly, employees are concerned if they receive what they believe is an inaccurate or unfair appraisal.

An important question is how the employee should use upward communication to approach the manager when he or she believes his or her appraisal was inaccurate. First, the employee should wait until he or she can approach the manager with little anger or emotion. Second, the employee should review the criteria and the process for evaluation. Are the criteria objective indicators or subjective opinions? Does the employee have information relevant to the decision that was not considered? When all information has been gathered, the employee should ask to meet privately with the manager to discuss the relevant information and goals for the future. Emphasis should be placed on factual information. If it is clear the appraisal will not be changed, the employee should focus on the upcoming appraisal and what needs to happen to improve the rating. Perhaps the employee needs to provide the manager with more information during the appraisal period, or a process needs to be worked out so the employee is clear about the manager's goals and timelines. It would be wise for the employee to document the meeting, provide a copy of the documentation to the manager, and keep a personal copy. The employee should also make a point of tracking progress with the manager during the next appraisal period (Green & Knippen, 1999).

WAYS TO ENCOURAGE UPWARD COMMUNICATION

One of the most important factors for managers to consider in encouraging upward communication is to gracefully accept feedback, even if it is critical. It generally takes quite a bit of courage for an employee to approach his or her superior with negative or even neutral feedback. If an attempt is made, the manager needs to be careful not to react defensively or to attempt to discount the feedback. Even if the manager believes the feedback is inaccurate, he or she needs to accept it gracefully.

Upward feedback is also encouraged when employees believe their opinions are valued. One way to send a message that opinions are valued is to actively solicit employee input into decisions. Although management might not use, or even want, all employee suggestions, employees often have valuable ideas. The Egg McMuffin and all of its imitations originated from a lower level McDonald's employee (Zaremba, 1993). If managers avoid upward communication and suggestions because they do not want to face potential criticism, they can also lose valuable, often money-making or cost-saving, ideas. Reports of the communications taking place hours before the *Challenger* disaster strongly indicate that the problem was inefficient means of accurately conveying information from subordinate to superior.

Group interviews conducted by consultants or individuals not associated with the company can be very revealing. In one organization the first author consulted for, top management wanted to learn what employees believed were the impediments to their productivity. We did a number of nominal group interviews with employees at a variety of levels in the organization. The nominal group interview process consists of having interviewees respond to the interview question (e.g., What do you believe are the impediments to your productivity?). Interviewees independently record all possible answers to this question on paper. Then the facilitator records all group members' answers on a flipchart or whiteboard. When all ideas are recorded, there is time for discussion and clarification of the ideas. After all ideas are discussed and redundancies eliminated, group members rank their top five in order from most important (1) to fifth most important (5). Rankings are then compiled and generally a very clear picture emerges as to the most highly endorsed opinions. In this case, first line supervisors who did little to facilitate the accomplishment of work were seen as the most important impediment to worker productivity. Burdensome rules and regulations that were seen as overcontrolling were also noted as an important impediment to work accomplishment. This information gave us a good starting point for helping the organization develop a plan for improving productivity.

In soliciting input from employees, care must be taken to inform employees that although their opinions are valued, the requested change might not be the decision that is implemented. Many employees have opinions and they are not always in agreement with one another or with managers' imperatives. Employees need to understand that merely sharing a view or idea will not always result in the desired change.

Anonymous feedback solicited via suggestion boxes or anonymous surveys can also be useful, particularly when issues are highly sensitive or there is strong disagreement among groups about the most appropriate course of action. Anonymous feedback is also useful when there has been a climate of lack of trust, or perhaps when a new manager has been put into place.

Department or group meetings can also be useful for gathering upward communication. Too often managers hold meetings when they have information to communicate and tend to forget meetings also serve a purpose for those who have issues or opinions to share with the group or manager.

"Walking the job" can be a valuable mechanism for encouraging upward communication. Managers too often get glued to their desks and offices and believe walking the halls suggests the manager is bored or not busy. Popping into employee offices merely to ask "How are things going?" can lead to interesting conversations and can provide a mechanism for employees to get clarification about any rumors they have heard.

CONCLUSIONS

Clearly encouraging and embracing upward communication is one way to bridge the communication gap and to promote honest communication. We strongly recommend that managers realistically assess their reactions to upward feedback and the mechanisms in place to make it easy and desirable for employees to share their ideas and information. Communication in organizations needs to be two-way. Too often it is very lopsided in favor of downward communication and valuable input is lost.

TAKEAWAYS

- Having managers write development plans based on confidential upward feedback that is shared with their supervisors can help promote accountability for positive change.
- It can be useful for employees to share with managers their preferences for supervisory style and for the manager to share his or her expectations for interaction with subordinates.
- Managers can take steps to minimize or reduce cynical attitudes on the part of employees and to encourage open communication by being honest and explaining the rationale for decisions.
- Rather than arguing with an employee providing upward feedback, a manager should acknowledge the employee's opinion even if he or she disagrees with it.
- Suggestion boxes, open-door policies, and focus groups can be effective methods of encouraging upward feedback if they are taken seriously.
- Open-ended comments, as part of a multisource feedback process, should specify specific recommendations for change rather than mere criticism.
- Immediate negative reactions to negative feedback can be followed by negative change. Using coaches and follow-up with feedback recipients is recommended to minimize negative reactions and help recipients deal with feedback constructively.
- Managers need to be trained in how to effectively deliver face-to-face performance reviews.

5

Solutions to the Open Communication Dilemma

Deciding When and How to Give Negative Feedback

Feedback is good! Everyone wants feedback! The more feedback the better! This is the lore surrounding feedback, but generally it applies only to positive feedback. Consistent with Thorndike's (1927) Law of Effect, positive feedback is equated with reinforcement and is expected to result in more of the behavior being performed. Yes, everyone wants more positive feedback! However, negative feedback is equated with punishment in Thorndike's theory and thus people are far less likely to desire it. We know from chapter 2 that supervisors avoid giving negative feedback and often sugar coat it when they do give it. We also know that very few people enjoy giving others negative feedback, but providing negative feedback is often necessary to correct a problem situation or to improve individual performance. However, many questions arise having to do with when, how, and even whether to deliver negative feedback. This chapter addresses issues surrounding negative feedback and factors influencing its success when delivered. First, we address considerations that go into a decision about whether negative feedback is truly called for and whether it is likely to have the intended effect. Second, we discuss factors influencing successful delivery of negative feedback. Third, we provide some specific suggestions about steps to take in the delivery of negative feedback.

Ilgen and Feldman (1983), in their model of performance appraisal, suggested that when performance is appraised, the organizational context, the appraiser's information processing system, and the behavioral system of the appraisee interact. Fedor (1991) provided a feedback model that suggests that perceptions of the source and characteristics of the message itself, in combination with recipient characteristics, affect the way the recipient processes feedback. Both of these models suggest a combination of factors will influence how feedback is received and reacted to. For example, recipients try to interpret the feedback and their responsibility for the feedback and why it is being given. Understanding this, it is important for the feedback provider to first assess the "feedback situation"; that is, the message, the attitudes the recipient holds toward the provider, and the recipient's characteristics in assessing whether the feedback is likely to have its intended effect.

DECIDING WHETHER TO GIVE FEEDBACK

Latting (1992) suggested that the decision about whether to give corrective feedback should be based on (a) the supervisor's motives for giving the feedback, (b) the supervisor's assessment of his or her standing with the employee, (c) the employee's ability and willingness to take action, and (d) the organization's reward system. So, the first question asked by the person deciding whether to deliver negative feedback is "What do I intend to accomplish by providing this feedback?" The management literature has identified a variety of purposes, many of which are not merely to provide the recipient with accurate information. For example, a supervisor might give lower ratings than warranted "to get the recipient's attention," "show him or her who is boss," or to motivate the person to leave the workgroup or organization. If any of these are the goals of the feedback, it is our recommendation that other means be found to achieve these purposes rather than giving artificially harsh feedback. Negative feedback might also be used as retribution for some employee actions the supervisor was unhappy about (e.g., whistle-blowing). This goal is clearly unacceptable, and should never be used. The supervisor also might intend to provide feedback to motivate the recipient to improve performance in specific areas. If the goal is to provide corrective feedback, with the intent of improving the employee's performance or behavior, the provider can move on to assess the supervisor–subordinate relationship, the subordinate's ability and willingness to change, and rewards available.

As the feedback provider, consider the relationship you have with the recipient. If this is a relationship characterized by mutual trust and respect, the recipient will be more likely to receive the negative feedback as constructive. A study of discipline events (Charles, Atwater, & Goldman, 2007) revealed that when recipients had a positive relationship with their supervisor they were more likely to make positive changes and less likely to retaliate, regardless of how sensitively the discipline was delivered (e.g., with or without an apology).

Covey (1989) discussed the emotional bank account wherein the supervisor makes deposits when he or she delivers positive feedback or does considerate things for the employee. Negative feedback or criticism is an example of a withdrawal from the emotional bank account. If the bank account is in the red, negative feedback will not be taken constructively.

Take, for example, a teenager working in a restaurant. One morning, on her way out to work, the young woman is obviously upset. When asked by her parents what was wrong, the teenager complained that her supervisors never say anything positive, but rather, frequently find things to criticize, such as her earrings are too big or the color of her socks is wrong. This teenager is a loyal employee who does not call in sick and gets good ratings from customers and other employees, yet she hates her job and her supervisor. She is not likely to go the extra mile in this job and is likely to be motivated to quit (which she did). This is because her emotional bank account is bankrupt. Covey's (1989) recommendation is to provide three positive comments, or pieces of feedback, to every negative comment. If the supervisor's ratio is not even close, the negative or corrective feedback will likely not be considered seriously.

Is the receiver able and willing to make changes? In the preceding example about the food server, clearly she is able to wear the right colored socks and correct earrings. However, is she motivated? What are the rewards for obeying the dress code? In this instance the reward is not being reprimanded for inappropriate attire, or being fired. Perhaps greater rewards such as an occasional "Your uniform looks very nice today," when socks and earrings are appropriate would be more motivating.

CONTEXT

The context of the organization is also relevant to deciding how or whether to provide negative feedback. For example, providing any negative feedback at a time when employees are being laid off is troublesome. Even if the intention is not to send a message the recipient is next, it might still be interpreted that way. This often happens when products are no longer offered or organizational and departmental restructuring occurs. For example, at our college, a degree offering was eliminated. One of the staff involved in this degree program was very concerned that her position would be eliminated. The dean gave her great reassurance the position would not go away and her duties would be expanded into other areas. Nevertheless, when evaluation time came around, the dean was very hesitant about providing negative feedback, as this individual might interpret it as a "sign" she was going to be fired. This was a competent individual the college did not want to lose. In this case, the negative feedback was not urgent and thus was deferred to a later time.

FREQUENCY OF FEEDBACK

In addition to the Law of Effect, other psychological principles having to do with reinforcement are applicable to providing negative feedback. In chapter 3, we discussed the frequency of negative feedback. We specifically want to point out that the schedule of reinforcement is relevant. In terms of positive reinforcement, intermittent, unpredictable feedback is more likely to result in continued high performance than continuous or predictable positive reinforcement. With respect to negative feedback or criticism, continuous feedback results in desensitization and ultimately the recipient does not hear it or attend to it. Think about working in a noisy environment. When you first enter the work environment, the noise is very noticeable, but over time, you come to a place where you hardly notice it. Alternatively, employees working at a cinnamon roll shop must adapt to the sweet smell or they would never survive. The same is true for criticism or negative feedback. When it is delivered too often, people adapt to it and it no longer has the same effect.

In some jobs, especially mundane jobs where minor errors are frequent, performance has been shown to be better when a running total is kept rather than providing feedback after each error (Wade, 1974, as cited in Ilgen, Fisher, & Taylor, 1979). Imagine if Microsoft Word displayed an error message after every misspelled word. If you wanted to know how many words you had misspelled wouldn't you rather see an cumulative total per page, or per 10 pages, rather than after each error? Whether this type of feedback delivery works depends on the job and the frequency and severity of errors. Cumulative negative feedback (e.g., running total) will often result in better performance than feedback after each error, but the type of job obviously needs to be considered.

In a performance appraisal context, Ilgen, Mitchell, and Frederickson (1981) found that feedback delivered throughout the year makes the appraisal process more successful in improving performance. In a performance appraisal context, the running total is not advisable, but rather both positive and constructive feedback delivered periodically eases the discussion and improves outcomes when yearly appraisals are delivered.

FEEDBACK DELIVERY

The way in which the feedback provider delivers negative feedback also impacts how recipients react to it. For example, the extent to which the feedback delivery includes features such as concessions, justifications, and excuses can positively impact the recipient's intent to change behavior (Tata, 2002). Concessions include elements such as expressions of regret for the person's failure (e.g., "I'm very sorry your sales figures did not meet this month's goals"). Justifications include elements such as an appeal to the positive outcomes that could result from the event (e.g., "It is good this came to light now so you can get the problem solved before it becomes a bigger issue"). Excuses include blaming a powerful agent or lack of intention (e.g., "The boss is really cracking down on this now" or "I know you were unaware of the seriousness of this infraction"). Although we would not advocate blaming the boss rather than taking personal responsibility as the feedback provider, the point of this research is that thorough, empathetic discussion is more likely to result in changed behavior than quick "just fix it" conversations. Refusals or unwillingness to discuss the issue (e.g., "I really don't want to discuss this with you") had a negative impact on the recipient's intent to change. Tata's (2002) study also demonstrated that the more negative the feedback, the less likely individuals were to report intent to change behavior. So perhaps sugar coating to some degree is not always a bad idea. A follow-up scenario study (Atwater, Goldman, & Charles, 2006) found when the discipline event was the same (suspension), if the supervisor included an apology in the delivery, respondents reported perceptions of more interpersonal fairness, higher evaluations of the manager, and less anger following the discipline. The scenario read as follows:

> You have had 4 unexcused absences in the last three months. I am going to suspend you for a week in accordance with company policy. I'm sorry, I really regret that I have to do this. I realize this may pose a hardship on you financially. You will not be expected to show up for work next week. I'm really sorry.

This was compared to scenarios that expressed a refusal to discuss the issue as well as one suggesting that the individual was lucky only to be suspended rather than terminated. Although apologizing might seem trivial, we want to point out that when discipline must be administered, giving the recipient a way to save face, such as offering an apology, can help mitigate the negative consequences. Again, the apology is not to suggest the individual does not deserve the discipline, but rather that the supervisor is sorry to have to do it or sorry for the hardship it might cause the individual.

We would suggest on occasions when formal discipline needs to be administered, it might be advisable to present the discipline in writing as well so the poor performance and its remedy, as well as punitive action to be taken if not remedied, are spelled out clearly with little misunderstanding. If supervisors attempt to communicate such information only orally, it could dilute the seriousness of the situation or distort what really needs to be done as a remedy. If remediation requires a number of steps, it also serves as a reminder of the steps that need to be taken.

Baron (1990) conducted a laboratory and field study investigating the effects of destructive criticism. He studied potential interventions designed to decrease negative reactions to "destructive" criticism. *Destructive criticism* was defined as negative feedback that is inconsiderate, contains threats, attributes poor performance to the person rather than the situation, and is general rather than specific. The potential interventions designed to help mitigate these reactions were apology from the source of the criticism, attributing the causes of the problem to sources other than the negative intention of the individual, and the opportunity to express irritation toward the critic. Apologies by the source, as well as making attributions that were not internal, but rather that the task was difficult, were most successful in mitigating angry reactions and perceptions of unfairness from the recipient of the destructive criticism. In addition, those who received an apology or an external attribution were less likely to report that they would handle future conflicts using avoidance. Welcoming input from those receiving feedback has also been shown to be positively related to a number of desirable outcomes. Giving the employee the opportunity to state his or her side and to participate in the discussion has been shown to be important (Anderson, 1993, cited in Lizzio, Wilson, Gilchrist, & Gallois, 2003; Brett et al., 2005; Burke, Weitzel, & Weir, 1978; Nemeroff & Wexley, 1977).

Nemeroff and Wexley's (1977) studies also cautioned bosses against underestimating the importance of allowing subordinates voice. These studies also showed that bosses tend to overestimate the extent to which they effectively welcome subordinates' input. Brett et al. (2005) found that when discipline had to be delivered, supervisors who allowed "voice" from the recipients showed more improved behavior. Generally, participation from the recipient is called for most when (a) the threat to the employee is low, and the feedback is negative, but the consequences are not dire; (b) the employee has been with the organization for a number of months or years and has had a number of previous positive interactions with the supervisor; and (c) the employee is aware of the issue and has relevant knowledge about the issues to be discussed. That is, it is not merely denial or defensiveness. If the threat to the employee is high, as in the case of termination, there might be little reason to encourage participation (Cederblom, 1982).

The pleasantness with which the negative feedback is delivered appears to be an important factor in lessening the potential for negative emotional reactions and deterioration of supervisor–subordinate relationships (Greer & Labig, 1987). This is particularly relevant given that managers often wait until they are extremely annoyed before delivering negative feedback. This suggests it would be worthwhile to attack the issue when it is minor and the manager can still be pleasant.

Not surprisingly, when recipients believe they have been treated fairly interpersonally (e.g., the supervisor is attentive, respectful, and supportive), the acceptance of negative feedback increases and attitudes toward the supervisor are more positive. This again suggests that it is not merely what is said, but the way the interaction is handled by the supervisor that is important (Leung, Su, & Morris, 2001).

Delivering negative feedback in private has repeatedly been shown to have fewer negative effects than when done in front of others. Atwater,

Waldman, et al. (2001) studied observer reactions to discipline events. When observers were interviewed about witnessing a discipline event, many reported that they had bad feelings toward the supervisor or a lack of respect for the supervisor. Some also commented that they learned what not do to, but also how they would not handle a similar situation if they were a supervisor. In no cases did the observers report that they had increased respect for the manager based on his or her discipline behavior.

While in a meeting with six peers and her boss, the first author was the recipient of negative feedback. Following the meeting, all six commented to the author that they thought the boss was out of line and expressed their sympathy. Three peers even commented that the incident had reduced their respect for the boss. Although bosses might think they are sending a message to others when they discipline in public, they underestimate the extent to which they are also creating animosity between themselves and others.

Sequencing of positive and negative feedback is also relevant. Feedback presented in a positive–negative sequence was seen as more accurate than the same feedback presented in negative–positive sequence. This was very important for those with high self-esteem (Stone, Gueutal, & McIntosh, 1984). So, if the supervisor can find something positive to say to the recipient prior to delivering negative feedback, it can be helpful. For example, as mentioned earlier, complimenting the person on his or her great attendance record or dedication to the company over a number of years could be highlighted before the supervisor has to reprimand the individual for leaving doors unlocked when leaving.

When conducting performance appraisals involving both evaluative decisions (e.g., merit raises, promotions, demotions, etc.) and suggestions for development, many have advised conducting split-role interviews. Split-role interviews are conducted so supervisors have one discussion about salary or other outcome decisions and a separate discussion, months apart, where suggestions for improvement, necessary training, or other developmental issues are discussed. Employees' performance as well as attitudes toward their supervisor improved when the two types of discussions were done separately (Meyer, Kay, & French, 1965, as cited in Cederblom, 1982).

Type of Task

There is some evidence to suggest that the effects of feedback depend, in part, on the type of task the individual is performing, specifically whether the task is routine and repetitive versus challenging and novel. Not all jobs have developmental potential and attempts to provide developmental feedback might just prove frustrating to the individual and wasteful for the organization. Cummings and Schwab (1978) suggested that "maintenance" appraisals are called for when employees have been satisfactorily performing routine tasks for some time. This type of feedback is intended to maintain performance at acceptable levels rather than to improve motivation and performance. Remedial appraisals are used for employees whose performance has slipped to unacceptable levels. As a personal note, the first author of this book actually spent time working in a fast-food restaurant as a college student. She was not terribly successful at this job, largely because she was not "fast enough" in delivering fries and drinks. It is doubtful that feedback about her performance would have improved her ability to move quickly enough to serve customers more effectively. You can either get orders out fast enough or not, and when the behavior is learned, there is little feedback can do to improve it. This does not mean criticism will not have a negative impact due to its negative impact on motivation, but neither positive nor negative feedback is likely to modify these behaviors in a significant way.

Similarly, Jaworski and Kohli (1991) conducted a study with automobile salespeople. They learned that positive feedback (e.g., "My manager lets me know when he thinks I am producing good results") had both an informational and motivational function (i.e., expectations were clarified and the individual reported greater motivation to improve). Individuals who received positive feedback showed significant improvements in performance and satisfaction. Alternatively, negative feedback (e.g., "When I fail to meet his sales expectations, my manager indicates his dissatisfaction") had an informational function but not a motivational function, and it impacted role clarity, but not performance directly. That is, the person had a clearer idea about performance expectations following negative feedback, but performance did not improve. Perhaps this is another example of negative feedback resulting in lower self-confidence and reduced expectations for performance.

In Table 5.1, we outline the optimal sequence for negative feedback delivery when it is deemed to be necessary and likely to be productive.

We would now like to revisit some of the cases we highlighted in earlier chapters as well as new examples.

Case Example

Remember the case of Kathy we discussed in chapter 1. The manager had asked the team to include Kathy as a member but her performance and attitudes were problematic. The team decided to meet with her and provide their feedback about their perceptions.

The feedback meeting turned out to be a disaster. The short-term outcome was shouting, name calling, and tears among some group members, especially Kathy. The long-term outcomes included ruined relationships among Kathy and the task group members and the manager. As an example, Kathy would simply not speak to certain members for weeks following the meeting.

TABLE 5.1   Optimal Sequence for Negative Feedback Delivery

1. Private setting; face-to-face; pleasant tone.
2. Show respect for subordinate; prevent embarrassment; allow recipient to save face.
3. Give recipient the opportunity for input.
4. Maintain motivation and cooperation by acknowledging positive aspects of work or performance.
5. Prevent subordinate from getting upset. Invite reaction to your feedback.
6. Maintain credibility: Provide evidence rather than only hearsay.
7. Build commitment for improvement; invite ideas.
8. Show you value the subordinate: Comment on his or her ideas.
9. Give your ideas about how the subordinate can improve.
10. Build self-efficacy; let the recipient know that you believe he or she can improve.
11. Create a plan of action and a mechanism for monitoring progress.
12. Follow up to assess progress.

Note. Adapted from Lizzio et al. (2003).

Analysis

First of all, the group approach to feedback is inadvisable, particularly when three individuals, all of higher status and informal power, attempt to deliver feedback to one lower status individual. In this case, Kathy believed she was being ganged up on and rather than being provided with any constructive feedback she was merely being attacked. Second, the group, if they had analyzed Kathy's personal characteristics, would have realized that she was a person with low self-confidence in a position she was only marginally qualified for (because she was a relative of the manager and he had made the decision to hire her without input from others). Clearly she was going to feel threatened by feedback suggesting she was not competent or motivated. In this case, there were two more advisable approaches. First, it might have been wise, given the players in the case, to merely forget the feedback entirely and wait out the project and Kathy's involvement in it. It was not a work group situation, but rather a project with a finite end date. Alternatively, the individual in the group with the closest relationship and the least threatening position could have had a more informal discussion with her to assess her interest in continuing on the project and could have perhaps made some modest suggestions for changes in her behavior. This might not have been successful either, given the confidence issues and Kathy's tendency to feel threatened by any criticism, but it clearly would have been more advisable than the group approach.

Case Example

Recall the case of Frank from chapter 2. Frank was upset because his manager did not give him a bonus even though the criteria they had agreed on were not met. Frank's district manager met with Frank and let him know that his sales had not reached their target and unfortunately he would not be receiving a bonus this quarter.

After leaving the meeting with his supervisor, Frank had time to reconsider and sent a nasty e-mail to his supervisor indicating how disappointed he was that the supervisor had not taken into account all of his prior years of excellent performance, as well as the fact he had sold some products lagging in the marketplace. He was extremely disappointed that his supervisor had not awarded him the bonus, even though he had not exactly met the criteria. Frank, of course, did not believe others who had not met the target deserved the bonus. In this case, Frank attributed his lack of bonus to the poor judgment of his supervisor and his supervisor's lack of consideration of other factors in Frank's performance.

Analysis

Frank has a very high sense of self-esteem. He is not very receptive to any type of negative feedback. Instead, he makes an external attribution that it is his supervisor's poor judgment that resulted in his lack of bonus, rather than the fact he just did not meet the sales target.

Approach: Feed his ego. Remind Frank that because of all of his successes he is a role model for the department. Clearly this was atypical for him and surely he will get the bonus next quarter, but in the meantime he should set the example that the criteria apply to everyone equally. Just because he has the best performance history he should not be singled out for special treatment. Find some other way to acknowledge his contributions. Perhaps he can get special recognition for his lifetime contributions with the company at some upcoming ceremony, apart from this bonus process.

Case Example

John had worked for the county probation department as a Level 3 employee for 5 years. He was an outstanding employee and good organizational citizen, always willing to do whatever he was asked to do. He was quiet and rarely spoke up about issues or concerns he had. He was well liked by his coworkers and supervisor. When an administrative position was announced, John applied for the position. Although John was a good employee, he lacked the depth of experience in adult and child probation that was specified in the job announcement for the administrative position. He had only worked in child probation with no experience in adult probation. John applied for the position anyway and the hiring committee evaluated his file along with many others. Because his experience was insufficient, he did not make the list of potential candidates they planned to interview. John's supervisor was the chair of the hiring committee and had the job of breaking the news to him. She made a point of meeting with John before any announcements of the selected candidates were made public.

John's supervisor met with him and politely explained that although he was a valuable employee and skilled at his job, he was not going to be considered for the administrative position at this time. If he continued to do excellent work and expanded his experience base he could be considered for a position in the future. John listened politely but did not provide any feedback to the supervisor. The supervisor left the discussion believing it went well and John had handled the news well. The next day, to everyone's surprise, John submitted his letter of resignation from the probation department. He later informed one of his coworkers that he believed he had been mistreated in this decision. He also expressed his feelings of being treated unfairly to his clients. He really felt he had been treated unfairly after his many years as a good citizen and good employee.

Analysis

Clearly, the supervisor misinterpreted his nonverbal cues and because she failed to ask for any feedback from him about this decision, she was clueless that he was extremely angry and upset about the decision.

The supervisor should have realized, given John's demeanor in meetings and other interactions, he was going to be unlikely to speak up if he was unhappy. She clearly needed to ask him how he was feeling about the decision and to try to allay his feelings of unfairness and mistreatment. Could his resignation have been avoided? Possibly not, but the communication gap could have been significantly reduced had the conversation been less one-sided. John still might have resigned, but he might not have harbored such negative feelings about the organization, the supervisor, and the hiring committee had the situation been handled differently.

CONCLUSIONS

Giving negative or corrective feedback or disciplining employees is a fact of organizational life. In deciding whether to give feedback, managers should consider their motives, the employee's ability and willingness to change, the supervisor's emotional bank account with the employee, and the organization's reward system. What is in it for the employee to make changes (or to fail to make changes)? The organization's context also needs to be considered as in times of severe stress and uncertainty it might be best to delay the delivery of negative feedback if it is not critical. Feedback should be delivered in a pleasant tone, without anger, and with an apology for the negative repercussions it might have on the employee (e.g., financial hardship). Managers should consider the optimal sequencing of feedback delivery beginning with selecting the place and ending with follow-up on progress.

TAKEAWAYS

- Negative feedback should not be used manipulatively to motivate a recipient to leave the organization or as retribution for some employee action such as lodging a formal complaint.
- Managers should assess the emotional bank account established with an employee to ensure the bank account is not in the "red" if the manager expects the feedback to be used most constructively.
- Consider the organizational context (e.g., amid layoffs or restructuring) before deciding whether the timing is appropriate for delivering negative feedback.
- An apology for the impact of a negative discipline event (e.g., suspension) on an employee will lessen its negative effects (e.g., anger toward supervisor or organization). The apology is not to suggest the individual does not deserve the discipline, but rather that the supervisor is sorry to have to do it or sorry for the hardship it might cause the individual.
- Formal discipline needs to be communicated in writing so steps and consequences are clear to all involved.
- Pleasantness with which the negative feedback is delivered appears to be an important factor in lessening the potential for negative emotional reactions and deterioration of supervisor–subordinate relationships.
- Beware: The negative outcomes associated with public discipline outweigh the shared learning that might occur.
- Present feedback in a positive–negative sequence rather than a negative–positive sequence.
- Use split-role interviews separated in time for developmental and evaluative discussions.

6

Leadership and Nonverbal Communication

In a classic study of communication, Mehrabian (1981) estimated that 7% of the messages sent in face-to-face communication are in words and 93% voice, facial expressions, and body language. Although this esti- mate might be high (Birdwhistell [1970] suggested it was more likely that no more than 35% of the meaning of a conversation is carried by the words), it indicates that nonverbal communication counts a great deal. Interestingly, although we spend a great deal of time and effort teaching children and adults how to speak and write effectively, we do little to formally teach nonverbal communication. Largely it is learned by observation (Level & Galle, 1988). When nonverbal cues contradict what is said verbally, people are more inclined to believe the nonverbal message (Beebe & Masterson, 1990). Clearly, nonverbal communication has significant implications for the ways in which managers and followers communicate and the accuracy and effective- ness of that communication. *Proxemics*, the study of the symbolic and communicative role of spatial arrangements and variations in distance, is also important in manager–follower communication. In this chapter we review the important aspects of nonverbal communication and the ways in which it can enhance or detract from the communication gap.

NONVERBAL MESSAGES

There are at least six ways in which nonverbal messages (e.g., tone of voice, gestures, eye movements, etc.) interact with what we say to provide a coherent (or conflicting) message. According to De Vito (1993) these six ways are the following:

- *To accent*. We often use nonverbal signals to accent what we are saying, such as using hand gestures to accentuate our excitement or enthusiasm, or a frown or a raised voice to accentuate our displeasure.
- *To complement*. Laughing while telling a joke, or shaking one's head to reinforce agreement or disagreement complement our verbal messages.
- *To contradict*. Contradicting verbal and nonverbal messages are often unintentional. An individual who claims to be heavily involved in the group's work yet brings outside work to a meeting is using nonverbal behaviors to contradict what he or she professes. When people say they are not nervous but their hands are trembling, verbal and nonverbal messages are contradictory. Observers are likely to believe the nonverbal behavior because it is less likely to be consciously controlled and therefore more likely to reveal the truth.
- *To regulate*. Holding one's hand in the air to indicate that he or she wants to speak, or putting a finger to one's lips to indicate to another to be quiet are regulating functions of nonverbal communication.
- *To repeat*. We can use arm movement to motion "Let's go" while also saying to the group, "Let's go." We can motion "come here" with our index finger while saying "Please come here." We could put our hand up to indicate to someone to stop while saying that a discussion is over.
- *To substitute*. We can nod our head to indicate yes, shake our head to indicate no, or wave to indicate goodbye.

Let's look at some leadership examples of nonverbal communication that can widen or narrow the communication gap.

Scenario 1

An administrative assistant has forgotten to make an airline reservation for her boss's trip and now the only flights available have a 2-hour layover. In addition, the boss will miss the opportunity to have dinner with an old friend because the flight will arrive too late. The boss goes into the assistant's office and yells at her, shaking his finger and telling her how unhappy he is. The assistant is humiliated and on the verge of tears. The minute he leaves her office she calls a friend to complain about what a total unsympathetic jerk her boss is. Although the assistant realizes she has made a mistake, this encounter will do nothing to strengthen the relationship between the assistant and the boss. She will be afraid that any mistake in the future will lead the boss to react similarly. The nonverbal behaviors that accompanied the boss's displeasure have widened the communication gap.

Scenario 2

The boss goes into the assistant's office and calmly expresses his disappointment, but acknowledges that everyone makes mistakes. The boss reassures the assistant that he is confident she will be more careful in the future and gives her a squeeze on the shoulder as he leaves her office. The assistant feels terrible to have disappointed her boss and is grateful that he was so understanding. She makes a mental note to look for his favorite bottle of wine to bring to him as an apology. The communication gap is narrowed and the relationship is strengthened.

The words could have been exactly the same, but the tone of voice and the gestures said it all. Let's take an example of regulating.

Scenario 1

An employee is one of six employees in a group meeting. They are discussing a heated point with their boss. The boss begins to interrupt the employee who is disagreeing with him. The employee loudly proclaims, "Will you let me finish?" and puts his hand out toward the boss in a gesture to stop. This gets everyone's attention because the gesture and tone of voice appear hostile and disrespectful, yet the boss discontinues his talking and the employee finishes his point. In this case the employee's nonverbal behaviors have widened the communication gap as the boss will likely see this as rude or disrespectful behavior and will tend to avoid communication with this employee in the future.

Scenario 2

The employee, rather than talking loudly and using a forceful gesture, merely asks politely to be able to finish his point. Without the tone of voice and the gesture, the boss does not feel disrespected and the others around the table do not feel uncomfortable.

In either scenario, the individual gets to finish his argument.

As can be seen from these examples, nonverbal expressions can completely change the message of communication and the way others react to it.

Anyone who has seen the Meryl Streep movie *The Devil Wears Prada* can recount the nonverbal messages her character Miranda was known for. When reviewing a fashion line, a slight positive nod was good, two slight positive nods were great, and a smile was rarely seen but meant "out of this world." We see very few nods in the movie and the only smile we see is in the last scene. However, everyone around this powerful boss knew Miranda's nonverbal messages and what they mean. Interestingly, Miranda might exemplify the perception that outsiders have of Americans. Americans tend to be perceived as "loud, aggressive and competitive by world standards" (Andersen, 1991, p. 292). It is important for managers to realize that their nonverbal behaviors could lead those from different cultures to perceive them as aggressive even when they do not intend such.

There are a number of cultural differences in nonverbal communication worthy of discussion. As mentioned in an earlier chapter, nodding in some Asian cultures indicates understanding rather than agreement. Waving has different meanings in different cultures. In the United States, to wave hello or goodbye we use the entire hand waving side to side. In Europe this same wave would be with the palm exposed and fingers going up and down (De Vito, 1993). To complicate matters further, in Balkan countries such as Greece and Bulgaria, shaking one's head from left to right signifies yes while raising one's head means no.

Generally, nonverbal communication is emphasized more in high-communication-context cultures such as among Asians, Hispanics, and African Americans. Hall (1976) used the concept of context to explain cultural differences in communication styles. "Context is the information that surrounds an event; it is inextricably bound up with the meaning of that event" (Hall & Hall, 1989, p. 64). Anglos are generally low- to medium-context cultures and French and Japanese are low-context cultures. The lower the context, the less one should rely on nonverbal communication to express a message. In a high-context culture, tone of voice and facial expressions are very important to the interpretation of a message. Additionally, managers from low- and medium-context cultures need to be very sensitive to the ways in which those from high-context cultures will communicate nonverbally as well as the interpretations they might make of others' nonverbal communication. A slight look or nod that might have been meaningless could be interpreted as agreement or disagreement by someone from a Hispanic culture.

Touching

The appropriateness of touching varies by culture, gender, and status. It is generally more acceptable for women to touch women than for men to touch men, with the exception of a handshake or light touch on the shoulder or arm. Higher status individuals have more latitude in initiating informal touch than do lower status individuals. The manager can put his or her arm around an employee to indicate his or her approval or appreciation. This would rarely be the case in the reverse between an employee and the manager. However, managers should be aware that not all individuals see even informal touching as appropriate and they should be sensitive to cues indicating an employee's displeasure. In one of the work contexts the first author was engaged in, a male colleague had the habit of putting his arm around the women in the office and rubbing their backs. Every woman in the office found this unpleasant and an invasion of their personal space. The colleague was repeatedly asked to stop this behavior and eventually he got the message. (This example, although innocent on the part of the male colleague, actually verges on sexual harassment, a topic we do not take up here.) This demonstrates how what is intended as a friendly gesture can be interpreted differently by receivers.

It is important to be sensitive to cultural differences in perceptions of different types of touching. For example, it would not be uncommon for an American manager to give a light hug to an employee to show appreciation for something he or she had done. Similarly, Americans might touch one another on the arm to show agreement or support. However, in Korea, for example, these gestures would be seen as offensive. Koreans dislike being touched by others in a work setting. Germany is generally "nontouching" except for handshakes, and public displays of emotion are kept under control.

The Face

"The face can communicate more emotional meanings more accurately than any other factor in interpersonal communication" (Weaver, 1993, p. 298). Leathers (1992) contended that the face (a) communicates evaluative judgments of approval or disapproval, (b) reveals our level of interest in what the other is saying or what is going on, (c) exhibits intensity or how involved we are in a situation, and (d) indicates our level of understanding. The face is an instantaneous response mechanism and an efficient means for quickly conveying meaning.

Nonverbal behavior has been characterized as irrepressible. Try as they might, people cannot refrain from behaving nonverbally. For example, when people become fearful, we find that fear begins to appear on their faces involuntarily (cf. Buck, 1984). At times, managers might want to repress their emotions by trying to control their nonverbal behaviors. However, regardless of the emotion being felt and that which the person tries to covey, the nonverbal behaviors expressed will be interpreted. For example, if one tries to demonstrate neutrality on an issue, it might be perceived as disinterest.

Women are considered by most to be more nonverbally expressive than men. Their faces are more spontaneously expressive and when they try to exhibit a particular emotion they can do it more successfully than men. Although this likely serves women well in many social contexts, it might be a disadvantage in some leadership situations when it is socially appropriate to be distant and stern (DePaulo, 1992).

Smiling. Sex differences also emerge with respect to smiling. Men tend to smile less than women (LaFrance, Hect, & Paluck, 2003). A number of social motives have been associated with smiling. Greetings, persuasion attempts, and attempts to ward off others' displeasure are a few examples of social motives associated with smiling. If women tend to smile more, they might be more effective in realizing these social motives. However, this behavior and expectation on the part of others for women to be more cheerful and to display more positive affect could create difficulties when their leadership role requires them to deliver discipline or bad news.

In the United States, smiling is even an expected part of some jobs. As an example, smile training is included in the training for flight attendants (Hochschild, 1983). There also is a recurrent theme in the nonverbal communication literature that those with lower power smile more as a display of deference to those with more power (Keating, 1985). This might also partly explain the tendency for women to smile more as historically women have had lower status and power than men. Compounding this problem, in one study, smiling men were perceived to be less effective than nonsmiling men (Kierstead, D'Agostino, & Dill, 1988). Perhaps men are subtly trained that smiling is a sign of weakness. Nevertheless, managers, male or female, should be aware that smiling can ward off others' displeasure (Elman, Schulte, & Bukoff, 1977). For example, "saying it with a smile," or smiling when asking someone to do something unpleasant might help, but smiling should not be coupled with negative feedback or it could be perceived as sarcastic.

Eye Contact.   A direct, prolonged stare indicates either intimacy or aggression, both of which are messages managers generally want to avoid sending to followers. Typically, you should meet another's gaze about 60% to 70% of the time. However, individuals from different cultures view the importance of eye contact differently. In the United States, appropriate eye contact signals respect, attention, and integrity. However, Puerto Rican children are taught that eye contact with adults is disrespectful. This carries over into the workplace between employees and managers. Looking down is considered a mark of respect in the Puerto Rican culture, but could easily be misinterpreted by an American manager conversing with a Puerto Rican employee.

PROXEMICS

Proximity is nearness in place, time, order, occurrence, or relation. Proxemics is the study of the symbolic and communicative role in a culture of spatial arrangements and variations in distance (Hall, 1966).

Personal Space

All individuals have a perception of how close others can comfortably get to them in various situations. For Americans, intimate contact can range from touching to 6 inches, whereas social distance is generally 4 to 7 feet. Personal distance, which we use in conversation with others, differs by culture. For Europeans a comfortable personal distance is 9 or 10 inches. For Asians and Latin Americans a comfortable distance is about 12 inches. Contrast that with the comfortable distance for Americans of 24 to 48 inches (Pease, 1984). These differences in comfort zone can make relationships between managers and employees awkward. If an American manager is approached by a European employee and the employee keeps getting closer and the manager keeps backing away, the employee might feel rejected. This is not the message the manager wants to send, but rather her way of feeling comfortable in her space. Alternatively, if a Hispanic manager approaches an employee at a comfortable 12 inches, the employee could perceive this as too intimate or aggressive.

Managers' nonverbal behaviors have heightened importance because others are looking for clues about the manager's reactions and approval. You might be aware of meetings you have been in where certain people around the table always seem to be looking at the boss and "mirroring" his nonverbal behaviors to signal their agreement with him. This can be a method of impression management, that is, trying to get the boss to appreciate the employee and his or her support for the boss's ideas. The same can occur when the group disagrees with the boss and the group members can align their body language with one another to reflect their disagreement.

The following depicts how followers might overinterpret body language of their managers.

Imagine that you were a new sales representative giving one of your first sales presentations with your boss present. This is likely to be a bit nerve wracking. About two thirds of the way through the presentation, you look at your boss in the audience. He has his head in his hands and is shaking his head back and forth. You panic, believing that his nonverbal behaviors were in response to your presentation. Your nervousness is heightened and you are barely able to complete the presentation without fainting. After the presentation, you immediately go to your boss and ask him what you said that was wrong. He says he was not even concentrating on the presentation, he was thinking about something else. This demonstrates a valuable lesson about how managers need to be attentive to their nonverbal behaviors as they are likely to be overanalyzed.

Status, Space, and Communication

In our culture, space equates to power. In many government agencies, a specific square footage allowance is provided for individuals at various administrative levels. Senior administrators in our culture are given more square feet, windows, and offices on higher floors. In France, by contrast, a high-level manager would sit in the middle of an office area because the central location allows him or her to better monitor employees (Chaney & Martin, 1995). Part-time employees share space. This allocation of space is one example of how space signifies power or status. The executive suite located on the top floor with windows on all sides and leather furniture communicates a different message of power and status than a 6-by-6 cubicle with a desk and file cabinet. Managers often sit at the head of a large conference table as a symbol of their leadership position. (Incidentally, one manager with whom we have worked rarely occupied the seat at the head of the table in meetings, but rather assumed a seat on the side to send a message of equality rather than superiority.)

Also with regard to space is the way in which the manager respects or disrespects employee space. An employee certainly would not march into a manager's office without invitation (at least knocking), but managers might not always be aware that employees deserve the same consideration.

The first author had an administrative assistant whose desk was located right outside her office. On occasion she would say, "Kathy, could you such and such?" without actually going to the assistant's desk with the request. Although Kathy could clearly hear the request, she brought it to the attention of the author that this was really quite disrespectful and she would appreciate either a phone call or a visit to her desk rather than (as she put it) hollering from the other office. Sometimes it is difficult to see how someone else views our behavior.

Office layout can also send nonverbal messages of openness or formality. When entering a manager's office and the only seats are those across from the manager's large desk, there is a sense of formality and status that cannot be broken down. Alternatively, if, when entering the manager's office, one sees a set of comfortable upholstered chairs arranged in a circular pattern with a table in the middle, the message is that this is a comfortable, friendly place for communication. Managers can widen or narrow the communication gap simply with office furniture and its arrangement.

Space is one of the many ways we can convey confidence, but body language is certainly another. Slouching versus standing straight with shoulders back is a clear indication of lack of confidence. Speaking without using hesitations such as "uh" and "um" signifies greater confidence. Qualifiers such as "Don't you agree?" and "in my opinion" also convey less confidence than making one's point without such qualifiers.

CONCLUSIONS

It is important for managers to be aware of their own nonverbal behaviors as well as those of the people around them. The body and the voice convey a great deal of the message. Defensiveness, anger, and disrespect can be created without the utterance of a word. Status, power, and confidence can be communicated nonverbally and these nonverbal cues can either support or contradict words and position. A clear understanding of the importance of nonverbal communication should narrow the communication gap between managers and those in their environment.

TAKEAWAYS

- Nonverbal behaviors (tone of voice, gestures, body language) convey more to the person a manager is communicating with than do the actual words he or she uses.
- Nonverbal expressions can completely change the message of communication and how others react to it.
- Managers need to be sensitive to cultural differences in nonverbal communication such as the appropriateness of touch and eye contact.
- Managers need to be sensitive to employees' needs and desires for personal space and the cultural differences in comfort with differing degrees of closeness.
- Managers can widen or narrow the communication gap simply with the type of office furniture and its arrangement.

The Open Communication Dilemma in Organizational Information Sharing

7

Creating an Environment of Open Communication

As shown previously in this book, open communication is an obvious challenge for leaders in their one-on-one relations with followers. Knowing if, when, and how to openly communicate performance and related concerns to followers represent challenges for people seeking to be better leaders. We now turn our attention to the communication of organizational issues that go beyond the performance of the individual follower. Instead, the information pertains to the myriad of events going on in the organization to which the manager might have access because of his or her position in the hierarchy. The nature of the information will change as compared to what we have already considered in earlier portions of this book (i.e., performance feedback to followers). However, the challenge or dilemma remains essentially the same: if, when, and how to openly communicate. Whether we are talking about one-on-one performance feedback or the sharing of organizationally relevant information, the stakes remain high for people in leadership positions and their organizations. Effective communication is likely to result in a committed and motivated workforce, creative problem solving, and innovation. Unfortunately, ineffective communication can have opposite, deleterious effects. That is, poor communication can result in a demotivated and unempowered workforce, as well as ineffective problem solving and a lack of creativity and innovation.

The purposes of this chapter are threefold. First, we consider the types of problematic organizational issues where decisions to share or not share information become important. Second, we provide an overview of relevant leadership theories and perspectives that can help us make sense of the complexities surrounding open communication. Third, we summarize what we know about open communication and information sharing. We now turn our attention to the types of circumstances in which information sharing possibilities take center stage for people in leadership positions.

WHEN DOES INFORMATION SHARING BECOME RELEVANT?

Managers are privy to much information and decisions people at lower echelons of the organizations do not necessarily see. To be sure, there is much information subordinates would rather not know or have to handle. On the other hand, there is information that is of relevance and concern to followers in terms of their own personal interests, or to ensure maximum organizational functioning and performance. A common denominator of such information is its association with change.

Change can reflect increased novelty or adaptation requirements for individuals, who can in turn experience high levels of uncertainty and fear of failure or loss of control. Because of concomitant fears of increases in work demands or constraints, change often evokes negative additional reactions (Ashford, 1988; Spector, 2002). It should not be surprising that people will tend to desire as much information as possible about impending change so input can be provided and personal actions taken in preparation for the change. We now describe three types of information commonly associated with change, about which employees will typically want information.

First, followers are interested in potential changes in policies, especially those dealing with rewards and resources. For example, they are likely to be desirous of information pertaining to any new policies or decision-making processes dealing with pay changes or work conditions. Indeed, such desire for information is likely to be intertwined with a desire to influence decision-making processes early on, before decisions are made. As such, it is difficult to consider information sharing without also taking into account decision-making processes. We return to this linkage to decision making in our discussion later.

Case Example

At a small university, all department chairs as well as faculty were employed on 10-month contracts. As such they did not accrue vacation leave, but were not officially obligated to the university for two months during the summer. The university president believed all department chairs should be officially accountable to their departments for 12 months a year (which few department chairs would dispute). To implement the policy change, department chairs received two yearly contracts (which they never had before). One contract was a 10-month teaching contract, and the other was a 12-month administrative contract. There was no discussion that this change would take place, the rationale for it, nor its implications. To make matters worse, because contracts had become a paperwork exercise, most department chairs signed them perfunctorily, not even noticing the contract change. The event that alerted the department chairs to the new policy was noticing on their pay stubs they had begun to accrue vacation leave. When the chairs asked the deans what this meant for things like getting summer grant money or teaching summer school, the answers varied from department to department. Needless to say, the chairs felt very out of the loop. Rather than understanding the purpose and appreciating the gesture of vacation accrual, many suspected sinister, controlling motives on the part of management. A much more positive outcome could have resulted with timely information sharing.

Analysis

Although management did not intend this to be secretive or sinister, appropriate attention was not paid to how and when to share information about the change. As a result, some chairs interpreted what was intended as a reward for their efforts as a secretive means to gain more control. Early information sharing would have minimized the negative attributions.

Second, followers would like to be kept informed regarding potential changes in existing technology or work-related procedures. Change can impact or disrupt work routines, and often such change is sprung on people without much warning or input. For example, when personal computers and word processing were introduced in the early 1980s, typists who lacked computer skills were fearful that their jobs would be eliminated, and for good reason. As another example, online air travel reservations have largely eliminated the need for travel agents. The relevant issue here is how, when, and to what degree information regarding such impending change is introduced to the organization.

Perhaps closer to home, you can probably think back on a time when a new work procedure or technology (e.g., e-mail system) was simply announced after the fact, although it was clear others were planning such changes far in advance. It is not unreasonable to imagine instances where you might have wondered why such information or plans were kept secret. If such things were not kept so secret, perhaps subsequent implementation might have been much smoother.

Third, and perhaps most important, changes involving actual restructurings are highly relevant to people in an organization. Not keeping employees informed about relevant information and decisions can lead to potential organizational problems. Restructurings can pertain to reporting lines or the actual reconfiguration of organizational units. When they occur, the work lives or work status of individuals can be dramatically altered, resulting in new assignments or job descriptions, physical relocations, and even dismissals or layoffs. Obviously, people would seek as much information, as soon as possible, if such changes were being planned.

As a special example, consider mergers and acquisitions. Morosini (1998) pointed toward the necessity of keeping information secret during the precombination phase of a merger or acquisition (i.e., before the deal is actually consummated). Morosini argued any leakage of information could lead to various entities such as the press reporting innuendo and half-truths. The end result is likely to be misunderstandings on the part of such important constituents as shareholders of the merging firms, or employees who might speculate wildly about what the merger or takeover might mean (e.g., layoffs). As well, the share price of the targeted firm is likely to increase.

On the other hand, when it has become clear that a company is a takeover target, it might be necessary for managers to take the lead in providing information to employees. If they fail to do so, rumors can be rampant, morale can be damaged, and some of the best employees might withdraw and leave the firm. Marks and Mirvis (1998) provided the example of First Interstate Bank in the 1990s, which was eventually taken over by Wells Fargo Bank. Prior to the takeover, Lilian Gorman, a human resources executive at First Interstate Bank in the 1990s, developed a human resources merger response plan that dealt with various contingencies, such as those pertaining to employee job security. The plan was widely distributed within the organization. Although Wells Fargo, as the acquirer, ended up using only part of the plan, at least it showed an attempt on the part of First Interstate management to keep employees informed about issues relevant to them.

We consider in more detail reasons for limiting information disclosure when pursuing actions, such as a potential merger or acquisition, in the next chapter. We also consider likely outcomes when information is kept secret. Our attention now turns toward perspectives on managerial behavior and leadership that will help provide insight as to why information is kept secret, as well as the potential value or liability of information disclosure. Should people in leadership positions be more open in their sharing or disclosure of information to followers? The following discussion should help shed light on this important question.

MANAGERIAL AND LEADERSHIP PERSPECTIVES

A number of perspectives in the managerial and leadership literatures are relevant to an understanding of open communication and information disclosure on the part of individuals in leadership positions. These perspectives can help us make sense of the challenges involved in whether or not, when, and how to openly disclose information to followers, as well as other individuals such as clients and customers. Next we review the following: (a) Yukl's (1998) framework for classifying managerial and leader behavior; (b) leader-member exchange (LMX) theory; (c) participative leadership theory; (d) emerging perspectives of shared leadership, stewardship, and servant leadership; and (e) emerging theory on leader integrity.

Informing as an Aspect of Managerial Practice

Yukl (1998) considered the various key roles associated with leadership. One such role was *informing*, defined as disseminating relevant information about decisions, plans, and activities to people who need it to do their work. Another related role is consulting, which involves checking with people, or involving them, before making decisions or changes that could affect them. Yukl (1998, 2002) suggested that the informing role could involve a variety of different communication media, including telephone, written reports or memos, e-mail, and face-to-face meetings. His research suggested that keeping followers more informed tends to result in leader and group effectiveness.

Other authors have also touted the value of the information-sharing role. For example, Pfeffer and Veiga (1999) stated that information sharing is an essential component of high-performance work systems. They pointed to the sharing of such information as financial performance, strategy, and operational measures. As noted by John Mackey, CEO of Whole Foods Markets, "If you're trying to create a high-trust organization ... an organization where people are all-for-one and one-for-all, you can't have secrets" (Fishman, 1996, p. 106). Yukl (1998) and Peters (1987) would agree that information sharing is the key to an empowered workforce that takes responsibility for solving problems and commits to organizational goals and change.

Case Example

In one organization of which we are aware, the CEO requested all department heads to prepare a list of the three lowest performers in each department by name. The lists were to be sealed in envelopes and handed personally by each department to the vice president. No one was to know of this request. The fact that the three lowest performers could be above satisfactory was not considered. A number of department heads questioned the reasoning and appropriateness of this request, as well as what the information would be used for. No answers were provided. Some department heads refused to comply with the request, knowing they could be fired. Ultimately, as far as anyone in the organization knew, the envelopes never reached the CEO. Many people were concerned that the request would be leaked and lawsuits, or negative media attention, could result. Perhaps the merit of the request was questioned. Many of the department heads did wonder if the request was really appropriate, why the level of secrecy was necessary.

Analysis

When managers demand secrecy of their requests or actions, those of whom the secrecy is demanded need to understand the reasons for the secrecy to be supportive of it. Secrets are more likely to be leaked if those from whom the secrecy is requested do not believe it is warranted or necessary. Secrecy can also breed mistrust: Why must the request or information be kept secret? Is the request ethical? Might it unintentionally hurt others? Secret requests and demands for secrecy should be used only when absolutely necessary for the good of the group or organization.

Leader-Member Exchange

LMX theory is based on the larger social exchange theoretical framework prominent in organizational behavior research. LMX posits that the nature of leader–follower relations can best be understood in terms of exchanges in which such individuals engage. The quality of those exchanges develops differentially between leader–follower dyads over time (Dienesch & Liden, 1986; Graen & Uhl-Bien, 1995; Sherony & Green, 2002). Further, this differential development of exchanges can be based on aspects of match, or mismatch, between leaders and followers. Examples include the extent to which they align in terms of demeanor, values, work ethic, styles, and so forth.

When higher quality exchanges develop, one would expect to see a greater degree of mutual liking, loyalty, and support between leader and follower (Dienesch & Liden, 1986). These followers are referred to as the leader's in-group. In addition, followers in higher quality exchanges should enjoy advantageous rewards, such as more satisfying positions (Graen, Wakabayashi, Graen, & Graen, 1990) and more favorable performance evaluations (Gerstner & Day, 1997). We would further argue that such followers should also be privy to a higher degree of information exchange. That is, the leader will feel more confident in divulging even sensitive information because of the trust and loyalty placed in a high-quality exchange follower. A key reason people in leadership positions might feel uneasy in sharing information with followers is that they are not sure what the followers might do with it. On the one hand, followers could use the information to make better decisions, perform their jobs better, and help build the organization. On the other hand, followers could potentially use the information in less constructive ways, such as using it as a political weapon to serve their narrow self-interests. For example, information pertaining to a major restructuring of the firm could be fed to the local media prematurely, only serving to hurt public relations. Followers in the leader's in-group would more likely be trusted to use such information in a more constructive manner, and with discretion.

A different picture emerges in lower quality exchanges. These leader–follower relationships also can emerge, and followers in such exchanges tend to be considered as the leader's out-group. Lower quality exchanges are characterized by less mutual liking, loyalty, and support. Followers tend to perform to minimally meet requirements, and they receive close supervision from the leader, as well as fewer rewards. We expect followers who engage in such lower quality exchanges will be less likely to receive a high degree of information from the leader. That is, the leader will feel less confident in presenting sensitive information to out-group members because of a lack of trust. The leader might worry such information could be leaked to others or used in ways that could either harm the leader or the organization. For example, valuable new technical insights developed by in-group members might not be shared with those in the out-group for fear of the new technology being leaked outside of the organization to competitors.

In addition to out-group membership driving a lack of information sharing, the reverse can also be the case. That is, when important the manager does not share important information with followers, he or she might promulgate out-group development. In other words, followers who might not have had a propensity toward lower quality exchanges with the manager might move in that direction because of how a lack of information sharing signals less trust and faith in followers. We return to the implications of such behavior later.

Theory X and Y and Leadership

Theory X and Y represent assumptions about the nature of people. Theory X represents a pessimistic view of human nature and holds that most people and employees in particular tend to be lazy, lack ambition, and require supervision to keep them in line (McGregor, 1960, 2006). Theory Y, on the other hand, assumes people are capable of and willing to exercise self-control and self-direction (McGregor, 1960, 2006). These assumptions about human nature also influence how and what managers communicate to employees. Those with a Theory X assumption are less likely to believe in sharing information, are less likely to trust their employees to use information constructively, and are more likely to try to keep an eye on employees.

Case Example

A top manager believes that an existing flex-time policy could detract from the ability of the organization to serve customers and accomplish its goals because, as it has turned out, too many people are working long days and taking Monday or Friday off. She realizes flex-time is consistent with family work–life balance, and reducing commuting, but she would like a number of employees to choose to give up their flex hours. Because she doesn't trust that anyone will voluntarily change their hours to better serve the organization, she sends out a communication suggesting the flex-time policy will no longer be in effect. She realizes some people need flex-time to keep their jobs and actually doesn't plan to eliminate it entirely, but she thinks if it appears that flex-time is going away, only those who really need it will insist. Had this been a manager with more of a Theory Y orientation, she could have made an appeal to employees, highlighting what the issues were and why it was important to better serve customers. The employees then could have been asked to figure out a way to plan work schedules so that some of them could keep their flex hours, or they could alternate flex hours to solve the problem.

Analysis

This Theory X manager did not trust that employees would be willing to solve the problem in a responsible manner. Thus, she implemented her own problem-solving strategy that involved withholding her concerns and using a manipulative means to handle it. A likely result is less trust and commitment between employees and management in the organization.

Participative Leadership

Traditionally, participative leadership has been the subject of much research in organizations (e.g., Cotton, Vollrath, Froggatt, Lengnick-Hall, & Jennings, 1988; Leana, Locke, & Schweiger, 1990), as well as models of effective leadership (e.g., Vroom & Jago, 1988). In recent years, managers in organizations have increasingly been encouraged to practice more participative forms of leadership with regard to both day-to-day decision making (Vroom, 2000) and longer term strategies and visions (Nanus, 1992; Sagie, 1997; Senge, 1990). However, we stress that the term *encouraged* does not necessarily mean high degrees of participation are actually in place in organizations, as evidenced by our earlier example. Indeed, as described later and in the next chapter, there might be strong forces in play keeping managers from being truly participative, as well as informative, in their approach to leadership.

A number of reasons account for the trend toward, or at least the encouragement of, participative practices. First, for years, management gurus have encouraged such leadership behavior (e.g., Peters, 1987). Second, academic theory and research have pointed in the direction of the value of participation (Cotton et al., 1988; Vroom, 2000). Third, employees increasingly expect participation in the decisions that affect them and their work settings. It follows that managers have been increasingly developed and acculturized through their organizational experiences to be more accustomed to the concept of participation (Vroom, 2000), including its potential value and desire on the part of followers to provide input into decision making. Differences do exist across societal

and organizational cultures with regard to norms pertaining to participative leadership (House et al., 2004). At the same time, the value
and desirability of such leadership among managers in many cultural
contexts has increased generally (Yukl, 2002). In addition, the punishment or negative outcomes that can result from poor decisions will tend
to encourage managers to seek out participation from others, both as
a way to improve the quality of decisions, and also as a way to spread
responsibility and ownership to others.

We propose that more participative forms of leadership run hand in
hand with information sharing. Decision making is the activity that
forms the basis of participative leadership. In turn, effective decision
making can only be accomplished when the people involved have
access to relevant information. Indeed, it might be impossible to be an
authentic, participative leader, while holding back information relevant
to those who are participating. In short, more participation will inevitably lead to more information sharing between leaders and followers.

The preceding discussion would suggest an actual trend toward more
participative forms of leadership, and overall, such is probably the case.
As described later, the case for participation has become even stronger
in recent years with trends toward such leadership approaches as shared
leadership, stewardship, and servant leadership. However, before we
consider such approaches or trends, we should first acknowledge forces
at play that might tend to reduce participative leadership, and hence,
information sharing.

Although the encouragement toward participation has been strong,
at the same time, leaders have been cautioned to use situational or contingency approaches to leadership. For example, the Vroom and Jago
(1988, 1995) contingency model would suggest that leaders should only
allow for maximum participation under the following conditions:

- Follower commitment is essential to carrying out a decision,
  and there would be little commitment if the manager made the
  decision exclusively.
- The manager has a deficiency of information to make the decision alone (i.e., followers could add to the manager's information
  or expertise).
- Followers support the organization's goals or objectives with regard
  to the decision.

Some recent research has questioned the utility or validity of using
such contingency models (Vecchio, Bullis, & Brazil, 2006). One problem is that managers are likely to have a tendency to underrate such
factors. In other words, they will tend to believe followers will carry out
decisions, regardless of whether they are involved and information was
shared. They will also tend to believe they are the ones who have the
sufficient information or expertise to make decisions, and that followers

might not be very supportive of the organizational objectives intertwined with decisions. In LMX terms, managers might have a tendency to over-estimate the extent of their out-groups, especially when it comes to choices regarding the extent of participation in decisions. This problem was illustrated in our earlier example regarding flex-time scheduling. At the same time, we should note that the Vroom and Jago (1988) model actually encourages a more developmental tact whereby, time permit-ting, managers are pushed toward using a more participative stance in their decision making.

So what's the upshot of such situational or contingency thinking with regard to participation? On the one hand, it might drive managers away from the allowance of full participation in decision making on the part of followers. On the other hand, in accordance with the push toward more participation in organizations (Yukl, 1998, 2002), and the devel-opmental model suggested by Vroom and Jago (1988), managers will also realize it might not be practical or even possible to be autocratic or authoritarian. Autocratic leadership goes beyond decision making (and whether or not to include followers in such processes) in that it involves attempts at dominating followers, forcing values and opinions on them, and so forth. Such leadership practices have become increas-ingly unpopular in recent times.

Managers often settle for middle ground and what Vroom and Jago (1988) would refer to as *consult*. In other words, they present an issue or problem to followers (either individually or in a group), get their ideas and suggestions, and then go back and make decisions on their own. As such, managers can limit the scope of information divulged and maintain control of the decision-making process, rather than truly sharing it with followers. However, to use the process of consultation, as defined by Vroom and Jago (1988), implies only marginal participation and infor-mation sharing. Yet organizations often encourage such superficial, and perhaps even symbolic, approaches because they provide the appearance of participation, while keeping control in the hands of management. In addition, allowing true participation can create expectations on the part of followers that their input will implemented, which can be problem-atic for the manager if followers' input turns out to be unacceptable. Consultation is much safer. Nevertheless, followers might want, and believe they deserve, a much higher degree of participation on a con-sistent basis. We next consider specific models of leadership that take participation, and information sharing, to a higher level.

Shared Leadership, Stewardship, and Servant Leadership

In recent years, a number of approaches to the understanding of effective leadership have been put forth in the literature with a common denomi-nator of power equalization. Specifically, each stresses the exchange of power and authority between those in leadership positions and those in follower positions, at least in reference to the traditional organizational chart. For example, Pearce and Conger (2003) defined *shared leadership* "as a dynamic, interactive influence process among individuals in groups for which the objective is to lead one another ... the influence process involves more than just downward influence on subordinates" (p. 1). As such, shared leadership involves an influence process broadly distributed among a set of individuals, rather than being only concentrated in the hands of a single, hierarchical leader. Pearce and Conger pointed toward evidence that a shared leadership approach is likely to produce more effective outcomes, compared to traditional top-down management, especially in more knowledge-based jobs.

Similarly, the concept of stewardship implies a partnership assumption whereby power and control shift away from formal leaders to the employees of a firm (Block, 1993; Davis, Schoorman, & Donaldson, 1997). Specifically, stewardship involves localizing decisions and power closest to those who do the work and serve customers, as well as organizing into semiautonomous teams. As noted by Daft (2005), stewardship would suggest managers who are honest with employees, "neither hiding information nor protecting [employees] from bad news" (p. 229). Southwest Airlines provides a good example of both shared leadership and stewardship. The emphasis is on serving customers by pushing decision making down to the levels where customers can best be served, as well as a "we" (as opposed to "I"), team-based culture.

Servant leadership takes stewardship one step further in that it essentially turns leadership practice and philosophy upside down. That is, servant leadership involves helping followers to grow and develop and essentially serving their needs as they, in turn, serve customers and clients (Choi & Mai-Dalton, 1998; Sendjaya & Sarros, 2002). Although servant leadership might seem like pie in the sky to many readers, Daft (2005) provided examples of managers from the business world who have essentially stepped into such a role, such as Robert Townsend of American Express and Robert Thompson of the road-building company Thompson-McCully. Both of these managers view their role more in terms of serving the needs of lower level managers and employees, rather than issuing directives or initiatives. Obviously, such a philosophy involves a high degree of trust in employees, as well as a willingness to take risks through their empowerment.

Perhaps more than any other form of leadership discussed thus far, servant leadership has the strongest implications for the free flow of information between managers and followers. We would expect a manager adopting the servant leadership role to simply provide followers with any information relevant to their personal welfare and their ability to be fully contributing members of the organization. As such, servant leadership would be viewed with a high degree of skepticism by those who see the need for at least some degree of discretion on the part of management with regard to the sharing of information with employees. We return to this issue in the next chapter.

Leader Integrity

The concept of leader integrity has been largely forgotten in past leadership literature. This is especially surprising because honesty, a trait certainly aligned with integrity, has been shown to be highly prototypical of leadership qualities (Lord, Foti, & DeVader, 1984). That is, when people think of the term *leader* or *leadership*, they are highly likely to think about honesty and integrity.

More recently, researchers are indeed paying attention to the topic of integrity, perhaps due, in part, to recent corporate scandals that are clearly characterized by a lack of integrity on the part of high-level leaders. For example, Thomas, Schermerhorn, and Dienhart (2004) demonstrated how a lack of integrity or ethics is often associated with such costs as government fines, attorney and audit fees, and investigative costs. These costs may be difficult to identify because they are buried within the overall costs of doing business. Moreover, less quantifiable costs could be associated with a lack of integrity, such as those due to loss of firm reputation, lower employee morale, and employee turnover or difficulty in recruiting top talent.

But what exactly is leader integrity, and how is it relevant to open communication on the part of leaders? A number of definitions and characterizations have emerged in the literature. For example, Parry and Proctor-Thomson (2002) defined leader integrity in terms of "commitment in action to a morally justifiable set of principles and values" (p. 76). In their measure of leader integrity at the supervisory level, Craig and Gustafson (1998) included such things as telling the truth, lack of vindictiveness and hypocrisy, and giving credit to others. Furthermore, various authors suggest that integrity and transparency are keys to being authentic as a leader (Avolio, Gardner, Walumbwa, Luthans, & May, 2004; Bass & Steidlmeier, 1999).

None of the preceding definitions or measures specifically link leader integrity and open communication. However, some recent research would suggest that integrity and open communication are indeed closely aligned. Waldman et al. (2006) have been engaged in a line of research examining the nature of leader integrity, its antecedents in terms of leader values, and its outcomes. Their research is based on an ongoing study of managers from approximately 600 firms in 15 countries around the world. One of the more interesting findings from this work is that leader integrity appears to be a multifaceted construct encompassing a range of behaviors and attributions (see Waldman et al., 2006). So as one might expect, integrity involves such things as keeping one's word and not lying. However, it also involves being open and sharing or disclosing critical information to followers. In other words, information sharing appears to be central to being seen as a leader who has integrity. On the other hand, the hoarding of information results in perceptions of a leader who is lacking in integrity. Moreover, in line with servant leadership, leaders with integrity are seen as serving the interests of followers,

rather than just attending to their own self-interests. Favorable attributions on the part of followers are also associated with the integrity construct, including perceptions of selflessness, as well as trust in the leader
(Gottlieb & Sanzgiri, 1996; McKnight, Cummings, & Chervany, 1998).
Further, they are seen as having confidence in followers.

Although these aspects of integrity could seem somewhat disparate,
they actually tell a quite coherent story. When managers share critical
information with followers, they are simultaneously seen as being honest
and having confidence in those followers. Further, the sharing of information goes along with selflessness and not using information for one's
own personal power or good fortune. The end result is that followers
have a high level of trust in managers they view as having integrity.

Consider an example of how information secrecy could foster the
perception on the part of employees that the manager lacks integrity.
Specifically, talks between one manager and a manager from another
unit of the organization are occurring that could potentially result in
some sort of internal restructuring or even merger between the two
units. Instead of fully disclosing information regarding the nature of the
proposed restructuring or its potential implications, attempts are made
to keep the talks secret from employees. If employees find out about
the talks (and in all likelihood, they will), there is a high likelihood
they might attribute two things to their manager, neither of which is
positive. First, they will attribute that the manager does not have confidence in them. In other words, they will perceive that he or she does not
trust that the manager will use the information constructively, or that
their input is of any real value. Second, employees might attribute that
the manager is not sharing information, or allowing for participation,
out of self-interests. That is, by keeping the talks secret, the manager
can pursue an agreement (or no agreement) that would only be in his
or her self-interests, or those of a subgroup of employees. The upshot is
that the information secrecy only serves to lessen perceptions of integrity on the part of the manager, especially if the results of the talks are
perceived to have not led to a productive outcome.

We should note there are some mitigating factors that serve to complicate information sharing and perceptions of integrity. For example,
the manager might only share information with his or her in-group, or
in the case of a higher level leader, only share information with his or
her immediate management team, who, in turn, are instructed to keep
the information secret from lower level employees. The dilemma for the
manager is determining with whom and how much information should
be shared. Solutions to this dilemma are considered in later chapters.
For now, suffice it to say that perceptions of integrity will always be
threatened when one or more followers believes information should
have been shared, but was not.

Even if a person in a leadership position was not so concerned about
being viewed as having integrity, and thus not concerned about the
sharing of critical information, there are other reasons to be worried

about the level of integrity on the part of managers. First, as noted previously, the work of Thomas et al. (2004) would suggest that a lack of integrity can indeed be costly for organizations. Second, Waldman et al. (2006) and Sully, Waldman, Washburn, and House (2006) have found that leader integrity is associated with some important outcomes, in addition to financial performance: (a) the optimism and hope for the future expressed by followers, and (b) the extent to which followers use socially responsible values in their own decision making. In short, the sharing or disclosing of critical information appears to be part of an integrity construct related to important outcomes for followers and the firm as a whole.

Some other findings from the work of Sully et al. (2006) show how the values of managers can serve as antecedents in the determination of whether managers will practice, and be seen by followers as having, integrity. Managers with strong values emphasizing the importance of being socially responsible are viewed by followers as having high integrity, as well as being inspirational and visionary. Such values emphasize the importance of employee relations and development, treating minorities with dignity and respect, making decisions that will not harm the physical environment, and serving the needs and interests of customers. On the other hand, values emphasizing profit maximization, cost control, and sales volume are negatively associated with perceptions of leader integrity on the part of followers. Taken in total, these findings would suggest that, somewhat ironically, managers who have a predominant concern for profits will find that such values become unrequited in terms of ultimately resulting in profits and other outcomes. Moreover, these findings cast doubt on the efficacy of a strong economic view of the firm, as well as agency theory, which would suggest that mechanisms should be developed to ensure that managers stress profits above all other concerns (Ghoshal, 2005; Jensen & Meckling, 1976).

To summarize, the work of Waldman and colleagues (2006) has three key implications. First, it suggests that information sharing is central for a manager to be considered as one with integrity. People in leadership roles who are seen as having integrity tend to be those who share critical information that followers seek or to which they want to be privy. Second, values of managers tend to be a determining factor in others' perceptions of integrity. Specifically, strong socially responsible values, rather than profit maximization values, appear to foster perceptions of integrity. Third, leader integrity has a number of positive outcomes for the organization.

TAKING CAUTION FROM LEADERSHIP THEORY

In previous chapters, we have noted problems with open communication in providing performance feedback to followers. Accordingly, we have urged caution in the feedback sharing process. In a similar vein, despite the preceding discussion, there is at least some need to take caution from leadership theory with regard to the sharing and disclosure of organizational communication in a completely open manner. First, as previously noted, the LMX perspective would suggest that some followers have not accepted the type of role that would generate confidence on the part of the leader that they can properly handle information disclosure in many instances. In other words, trust is a two-way street, and perhaps followers in the out-group are simply not trustworthy and capable of using disclosed information in a constructive manner. On the other hand, LMX theory would suggest the goal of the leader is to try to reduce the out-group by doing such things as sharing information, showing confidence in followers, and so forth. Thus, there may be a catch-22 with regard to information sharing: damned if you do; damned if you don't! However, the self-fulfilling prophecy associated with Theory X thinking would suggest that if you treat others like they can't be trusted, they will likely turn out to be less trustworthy. Perhaps the leader could try sharing information that would not be too troubling if leaked, simply to demonstrate trust in out-group members as a first step toward more broad-based information sharing.

Perhaps guidance can also be found in situational or contingency views of employee participation in decision making. Such views would suggest that for some types of decisions (e.g., relatively unimportant ones), followers would rather not be burdened, and thus would rather not be inundated with information pertaining to the decision (Vroom & Jago, 1988). In other words, for such minor or irrelevant decisions (i.e., irrelevant to the followers), they would just prefer the manager handle it himself or herself without disclosing much information. Furthermore, for some decisions, employee commitment might not be necessary, and employees might not share the greater organizational concerns or goals. Hence, their involvement in the decision making, and the sharing of information, could at best be minimal.

At the same time, such situational or contingency thinking on the part of the manager could be problematic (e.g., Vecchio et al., 2006). First, as suggested earlier, what if this thinking is wrong or not shared by followers? In other words, what if followers view the situation much differently such that, for example, the decision is indeed important or relevant to them? As another example, what if followers feel they do indeed share organizational goals, but just view the potential accomplishment of those goals in a somewhat different manner than the manager? In both instances, followers would perceive that more involvement in decision making, as well as the sharing of information, would be warranted.

In sum, although there might be some reason to take caution from leadership theories with regard to information sharing and disclosure, there are clearly counterarguments in both directions. In total, these theories suggest that despite the complexity in understanding the connection between the sharing of information and manager effectiveness, most theory and research would point in the direction suggested above: toward more, rather than less, information sharing.

CONCLUSIONS

We have presented a number of conceptual and theoretical perspectives in this chapter relevant to the sharing of information on the part of individuals in leadership roles. Although these perspectives vary to some degree, the overall implication is that, at least in theory, things seem to be moving more toward the manager as information sharer, rather than information hoarder. That is, such theoretical perspectives as stewardship, servant leadership, and leader integrity point in the direction of the effective manager as one who is more prone to inform and share information with followers, as opposed to hoarding or concealing relevant information.

Why is it that the information sharer will likely be the more effective manager? Our theoretical analysis in this chapter would suggest three key reasons. First, followers typically have a desire for more, rather than less, information. In short, they seek complete disclosure of information that might be of relevance to them. The information could pertain to very personal or individual areas of concern (e.g., one's personal job activities or responsibilities), or they could pertain to occurrences in the greater work environment (e.g., potential restructurings or shifting of product lines). By providing more, rather than less, critical information, employee motivation and empowerment will be maximized. Second, by sharing information, the manager generates trust, which can in turn lead to positive outcomes for the organization, such as organizational citizenship behaviors (e.g., doing things for the team or organization that are above and beyond those expected for the job; Pillai, Scandura, & Williams, 1999; Podsakoff, MacKenzie, Moorman, & Fetter, 1990). This is not to say information sharing is the only thing that generates trust. For example, Butler and Cantrell (1984) showed how manager competence is also a prominent factor in the generation of trust. However, trust is a complex phenomenon that at least to some degree hinges on the extent to which managers are seen as being information sharers. Third, information sharing might allow for more effective problem solving and creativity among followers.

TAKEAWAYS

- Ensure that employees clearly understand the rationale for imposed changes. Changes will be accepted more readily, even if employees have no input into the decisions, if they understand the rationale.
- If you are trying to create a high-trust organization, you can't have secrets or secretive decision-making processes.

- Authentic, participative leadership is incompatible with regularly holding back information and keeping secrets.
- Consultative decisions are often effective. Managers get ideas and suggestions and use them to make a decision.
- Shared leadership, where influence is broadly shared among a set of individuals rather than a single hierarchical manager, is likely to produce more effective outcomes, especially in knowledge-based work contexts.
- Information sharing is central to being seen as a manager who has integrity. On the other hand, hoarding of information results in perceptions of a manager who is lacking in integrity.

CHAPTER

8

The Mushroom Theory of Leadership

"Management treats me like a mushroom. They keep me in the dark and feed me a lot of manure—while somehow thinking that I will be happy and grow."

Maybe you've seen a quote similar to this one, along with a picture of a mushroom, posted somewhere in an organization, maybe even your organization. Certainly it would not have been posted at the entrance where the (supposedly) shared corporate values or vision are proudly placed, including values regarding the fair and respectful treatment of employees. Instead, it might be placed in someone's cubicle, a mailroom, or a bulletin board. When we speak of the mushroom theory of leadership with students or employees of organizations, it never fails to get a grin, chuckle, sigh, or look of sarcasm and even disgust. In return, we frequently hear about personal experiences that exemplify the mushroom theory. In short, it is not just a theory; it appears to be practiced in a wide range of organizations.

But does the mushroom theory only exist inside the minds of employees, the ones who are most likely to be the mushrooms? If you asked the ones most likely to be the mushroom farmers (i.e., managers), most would probably disagree that they keep their employees in the dark, at least with regard to matters of importance or matters they feel at liberty to discuss with employees. Certainly most managers would be highly offended that anyone could even think they feed "manure" to employees, even if it is just a metaphor. Does research support the existence of this theory? We performed a computer literature search on the mushroom theory of management. The result was a prompt that asked us to rethink our keywords, and then search again.

As discussed in the last chapter, leadership scholars and experts have consistently supported the notion of keeping employees informed and involved. Over the past 30 years, workplace interventions and models, from quality circles to reengineering to employee empowerment and stewardship, are based on employees not only having access to information, but assuming they will use information to improve performance. So why do we still see this slogan in cubicles and even as computer screen savers? The answer is that despite what managers say, and what management experts advocate, many employees still feel like mushrooms. Later in this chapter, we provide evidence for this phenomenon.

The overall purpose of this chapter is to examine the mushroom theory of leadership more closely. We have several goals. First, we take a close look at exactly what the practice of the theory really looks like. Second, we examine the individual factors that might induce people in leadership positions to engage in the practice. Thus, we continue to consider the leadership principles mentioned in the previous chapter as we also elaborate on the day-to-day pressures and other variables that could push managers in the direction of not sharing or disclosing information to followers. Such factors include characteristics or perceptions of the managers themselves, as well as characteristics of followers. Third, a consideration of the organizational factors, especially culture, prompting mushroom theory behavior is provided. Fourth, some data and case examples are included. Fifth, we consider likely outcomes when the practice of the mushroom theory is widespread in an organization. In short, we address the following questions:

1. What exactly is the mushroom theory in practice, and how do we know it when we see it?
2. What aspects of organizations and their cultures tend to encourage the mushroom theory?
3. Why do managers engage in such practices, and would they admit to it?
4. Why do employees think they are kept in the dark and fed "manure"?
5. How widespread is the phenomenon?
6. What are the consequences to employees, managers, and organizations for treating employees in this manner?

THE MUSHROOM THEORY OF LEADERSHIP REVEALED

Our understanding of the mushroom theory can be elusive in practice for one key reason: Like other psychologically based organizational phenomena, it is perceptual in nature. As such, it involves processes by which individuals (e.g., followers) attempt to make sense of their surroundings. Various cognitive concepts such as schema (Rumelhart, 1984), belief structures (Fiske & Taylor, 1991), and mental models

(Klimoski & Mohammed, 1994) can come into play. Without going into lengthy cognitive explanations, these concepts would all suggest that an individual will attend to stimuli and cues in his or her environment to make sense out of occurrences and observed behaviors.

Part of this interpretation includes attribution formation, which is an important phenomenon in our understanding of leadership processes in general (Yukl, 2006). For example, implicit leadership theory would suggest that people have stereotypes and prototypes about the traits, skills, or behaviors relevant for people they would consider to be "leaders" (Lord & Maher, 1991). Lord et al. (1984) found that honesty (or integrity) is the attribute people tend to associate most frequently with the category "leader," as opposed to the category "nonleader." Thus, based on findings we reported in chapter 7, a manager who is hoarding or manipulating information is likely to be perceived as lacking honesty or integrity, which, in turn, will foster the attribution of being a nonleader. Obviously, this is not a desirable outcome for a person serving in a leadership position.

So, given that the mushroom theory of management is largely perceptual, how might it actually operate in practice, and thus come to be perceived as such? In essence, the core of the theory is that managers simply do not disclose information that might be of relevance to others in the organization, especially those at lower hierarchical levels. Alternatively, they might manipulate the nature of information shared (i.e., feed them a bunch of "manure"), or provide information in an untimely manner, such as after a key decision pertaining to the information had already been made. Schein (2004) discussed the notion of information control to describe situations in which people in positions of leadership have to determine which information is appropriate to withhold, distort, share, or say truthfully. For reasons to be described later, they might see a need for information control, prompting them to engage in deceptive behaviors such as concealing facts or "spinning" the truth.

Take, for example, the scenario presented in chapter 1, in which the owners of a natural foods company had spent time in private meetings with a potential purchaser of the company. One option available to the owners was to simply keep such information secret, even to the point when the deal is legally consummated. Of course, this might not be possible because employees might observe the presence of outsiders, rumors could spread, and so forth. The owners might then be confronted by one or more organizational members (e.g., lower level supervisors or workers) and specifically asked whether discussions were ensuing with regard to selling the company to a competitor.

The owners would need to decide how much information they want to release and in what form. One possibility is to engage in overt deception (Grover, 1993). *Deception* can encompass a gamut of behaviors including distorting the truth, misleading others, or imposing a false idea to cause ignorance (Howard, 1992; Sims, 2002). Both lying and spinning are behaviors associated with overt deception. If the owner engages in overt deception, he or she would have two basic options. The first option would be to lie, intentionally delivering incorrect information to employees (Grover, 1993). The owner could say something like, "We have not been discussing the possibility of selling the company." Another deception option would be to spin the truth. Spinning the truth is deception achieved by adding, subtracting, or distorting information (Sweetland & Hoy, 2001). Thus, the owner might say something akin to, "The representatives of the other firm were here simply to see how we do things and talk about future collaboration projects that we are interested in getting involved with to see how we can mutually improve operations."

One might wonder whether there really is an alternative to engaging in practices associated with the mushroom theory. In the preceding scenario, the owners face a dilemma because of constraints of sharing information on account of strategic issues (e.g., ill will on the part of the potential buyer who might want to keep things "under wraps"), the potential of a backlash from employees, and the issue of sensitivity to those who might be impacted by the decision. So despite the potential benefits of sharing information, there could be some real harm in doing so. Despite this possibility, one potential alternative is to simply openly communicate, thereby totally circumventing mushroom practices. Alternatively, the owners could engage in deception avoidance. This behavior is different from overt deception. Whereas overt deception involves adding or subtracting facts in an effort to deceive, deception avoidance is characterized by controlling the conversation in a manner that allows the manager to restrict information flow without being directly dishonest. Although managers could potentially engage in both overt deception and deception avoidance behaviors, it is likely that they will lean toward one or the other strategy when faced with the type of scenario described earlier.

One simple deception avoidance option would be for the owner to state, "I do not feel comfortable discussing this issue at this time." Another might be to come up with an alternative solution that would be truthful, and even one that shows concern for the welfare of employees. As an example, the owner could introduce the idea of the employees banding together to purchase the company. In this case, he or she could respond by saying, "We are constantly entertaining interests from potential buyers. If this concerns you, I am willing to meet with employee representatives to discuss the potential pluses and minuses of a long-term employee buy-out, and what you all would have to do to make it happen." In this example, the owner would be able to restrict the information flow by avoiding saying that he or she is meeting with the competitor for a potential sale, and at the same time, a degree of concern for employees is displayed.

In sum, engaging in practices associated with the mushroom theory is not exactly an either–or proposition. There can be gray areas. Overt deception, not revealing information, and spinning are all in line with what we would term the mushroom theory. On the other hand, deception avoidance is more of a gray area that represents attempts on the part of management to shift communication to positive areas, while still restricting the flow of information to some degree.

The final piece to the mushroom theory metaphor is the hope that employees will be blissfully ignorant and productive as a result of it. Managers might really believe information secrecy or manipulation is generally the best course of action for employees and the organization, or they might fail to perceive that they are engaging in such behaviors. Either way, as we will see in the following discussion, this belief is probably more akin to blind faith or a pipe dream.

WHAT IS THE PROBLEM WITH TREATING EMPLOYEES LIKE MUSHROOMS?

In some ways, this question might seem rhetorical or obvious. The notion of treating a human being like a mushroom, even metaphorically, seems disgusting or obnoxious. But others might argue that in organizations, it is natural to think of information as being on a need-to-know basis. If you do not need to know (at least in the minds of people who have the information), then it should not be shared.

However, as discussed in chapter 7, there are a number of circumstances in which employees desire information and being involved in decisions that might pertain to that information, such as when change is occurring or being planned. To not reveal information could be threatening to their self-interests. For example, it could be threatening to employees if information is being discussed by upper-level management that could end up in work-related changes pertaining to organizational structure, job design, scheduling, and so forth. If decisions pertaining to such important matters are suddenly sprung on employees, they might feel like they are victims of the mushroom theory. Indeed, they might have such perceptions, regardless of the "manure" communicated about why the decision was made, why information could not have been communicated at an earlier date, and so forth.

From a psychological viewpoint, we see two problems here. First, employee empowerment can suffer when employees perceive that the mushroom theory is in play. Employees will get the message that information does, indeed, represent power, and thus they are not the ones who are empowered. Yukl (2006) listed a number of negative side effects of a lack of psychological empowerment. These include a lack of initiative and innovation, decreased optimism and hope, and reduced organizational commitment. We consider such outcomes further next.

Case Example

On Sunday, May 23, the headlines on the front page of the newspaper in a large metropolitan city announced that the governing board for higher education in the state was considering the restructuring of the university system in the state. Part of the proposal being considered was to spin off a branch campus of a large research university to become an undergraduate teaching school. The branch campus had prided itself on its research mission and graduate programs as well as its undergraduate education. The vast majority of the faculty and administration on the campus saw this proposal as a huge disaster. That aside, the way in which faculty were informed about this proposal was while drinking coffee and reading the Sunday morning newspaper. Needless to say, faculty reacted to the method in which the message was shared with shock, disbelief, anger, and fear.

As one can imagine, the faculty felt very much like mushrooms because not a word of the proposal, the reasoning behind it, or the likely outcomes had been shared with anyone but the university president (and a few select administrators the Friday before the Sunday announcement). Indeed, a number of faculty members believed that the President might have instigated the apparent divestment of the campus. The upshot was that many faculty members reported that they felt deceived, mistreated, angry, and disillusioned. In fact, some potentially new faculty members who had accepted job offers for the following fall withdrew their contracts with the university.

Over the course of the next year, task forces were set up, meetings were held, and so forth. After much hoopla, press coverage, meetings, and so forth, the eventual outcome was that the branch campus would simply remain a part of the larger university. However, damage to the trust that faculty members had in the board and the president might never be fully restored.

Analysis

The method used to share this information was completely unacceptable. For employees to learn that their organization might have a serious change of direction by reading about it in the Sunday paper is clearly unacceptable. This information should have been shared with administrators, who then shared it with the faculty and staff in face-to-face meetings where the restructuring process could be openly discussed. As it turned out, one faculty member commented, "We spent a year on a horrible roller coaster with countless hours spent reviewing potential changes and ended up just where we got on." If the potential splitting off could have been discussed with faculty as just one of many possible restructuring options, and if they could have been reassured that their input would be considered and that the decision was not a "done deal" as many expected, the damage could have been seriously reduced.

A second psychological problem is that the social identity of employees might suffer as they fail to identify with the collective the organization represents. Social identity theoreticians explain how group membership and identity shape, and are shaped by, the perceptions of people in groups and organizations (Hogg, 2001a; Hogg, Hains, & Mason, 1998). According to this perspective, groups are mechanisms for individuals to potentially maintain a distinct and positive personal identity. Furthermore, leadership practices can have an effect on the extent to which people identify with the groups or collectives to which they belong (Hogg, 2001b). We would argue when people perceive they are being treated metaphorically like mushrooms, their collective identity will suffer. Perhaps even worse, they might develop an antimanagement collective identity. In this case, they see management as the enemy, rather than as being supportive. Furthermore, we envision similar negative outcomes as might be the case with a lack of empowerment, such as reduced commitment to work toward team-based objectives.

ORGANIZATIONAL CULTURE AND THE MUSHROOM THEORY

Certain types of organizational cultures could help breed and reinforce norms and values pertaining to the practice of the mushroom theory. Kotter and Heskett (1992) described maladaptive cultures in terms of insular, political, and bureaucratic norms and values. These environments encourage distrust and self-interests. In such cultures, the practice of the mushroom theory could keep inadequate decision-making processes and political self-interests from being exposed. We can certainly think of numerous examples in the U.S. political arena where extreme measures were taken to keep information quiet. When these attempts are discovered, the outcomes are always worse than if the mistake had been acknowledged at the outset. In other words, the cover-up is more damning than the crime. In contrast, more adaptive cultures care deeply about a variety of stakeholders, including employees. Trust is more the norm, and accordingly, we would expect less practice of the mushroom theory.

Other authors have contrasted culture types that would seem to lend themselves to differing uses of the mushroom theory (Denison & Mishra, 1995; McDonald & Gandz, 1992). Specifically, an achievement-oriented culture focuses on the aggressive pursuit of specific targets and performance goals. In such an environment, managers might be encouraged to pursue initiatives and decision making in an authoritarian and quick manner, just to make sure things get done quickly, and the organization avoids "paralysis by analysis." Unfortunately, in the process, information might be withheld from employees, perhaps simply in the pursuit of being fleet. In contrast, a clan culture would put a greater premium on fairness and reaching agreement with others. It would make sense that such a culture would stress the open sharing of information, and thus, avoid applying the mushroom theory, but decisions will take longer.

WHY DO MANAGERS ENGAGE IN THE PRACTICE OF THE MUSHROOM THEORY?

As already suggested, the organizational context can encourage or discourage mushroom theory practices. At the same time, we recognize that individual characteristics on the part of people in leadership positions might induce behavior associated with the mushroom theory. In this section, we characterize these in terms of characteristics with a more negative or self-serving basis, versus those that are more positive and less self-serving. Although we make this distinction, it is also clear that in reality, both forces can be operating simultaneously. We further recognize that managers who practice the mushroom theory will tend to attribute their behavior to more positive motives or reasons, whereas the mushrooms themselves (i.e., employees) will tend to make attributions more toward the dark side; that is, they will blame management.

Negative or Self-Serving Behavior

Perhaps the most intuitive, and indeed most likely, reason for the occurrence of practices associated with the mushroom theory is that it reflects poor leadership. Specifically, it is largely associated with negative motives, self-serving behavior, and weak leadership, rather than a consideration of the common good of those being led and showing courage as a leader. We suggest three specific characteristics on the part of "mushroom farmers" or managers: (a) personalized power motive, (b) low trust or confidence in followers, and (c) being risk-averse and lacking courage.

Personalized Power Motive.   Most people in leadership positions, especially those who are able to achieve a high degree of effectiveness, possess a strong power motive (McClelland, 1985; McClelland & Boyatzis, 1982). People with a strong need for power find "great satisfaction in exercising influence over the attitudes, emotions, and behavior of others" (Yukl, 2006, p. 184). With that said, McClelland (1985) considered how the need for power could be delineated into two types: personalized power orientation and socialized power orientation. As just noted, at its core, the distinction deals with the nature of the leader's power motive, or the extent of an individual's desire to have an impact on others or one's environment (House & Howell, 1992). It also deals with the extent to which an individual has a strong responsibility disposition, or beliefs and values reflecting high moral standards, a feeling of obligation to do the right thing, and concern about others (Winter, 1991).

Although both orientations reflect a strong need for power, in the case of a socialized orientation, it is self-controlled or restrained and directed toward the achievement of goals and objectives for the betterment of the collective entity, rather than for personal gain (House & Howell, 1992).

Similarly, stewardship theory would suggest that steward managers will choose to act in the best interests of the organization instead of behaving opportunistically (Davis et al., 1997; Shen, 2003). In contrast, a manager with a personalized orientation uses power for personal gain, is exploitative or manipulative of others, and is narcissistic (Conger, 1990; Hogan, Curphy, & Hogan, 1994; Kets de Vries, 1993; Maccoby, 2004). Thus, he or she will act as an agent manager, putting his or her self-interests before the interests of the organization or other individuals (Fama & Jensen, 1983).

At times, hasty decision making can be perceived by employees as mushroom management because they were not consulted or involved. There might be pressures on managers to make quick decisions that do not allow participation, but these time pressures need to be clearly communicated.

It should be somewhat obvious how these differing orientations could pertain to the mushroom theory. We suggest a personalized power orientation lends itself to the manipulative use of information. Indeed, such individuals would personify the maxim, "information is power." As such, they would have a tendency to use information in a selective manner; that is, being exploitative in terms of to whom and when information might be shared. Their tendencies toward deception would cause them to try to convince followers that information either did not exist, or it could not be shared, when in reality such was not the case. In other words, they might attempt to feed followers a lot of "manure."

A different picture emerges for the manager with a socialized power motive. Such an individual would feel compelled to do "the right thing" by keeping followers informed in an open manner. Thus, we would expect him or her to feel a responsibility toward followers to "come clean" and share information that they might seek or find useful. Or, at the very least, such an individual is likely to engage in what we described earlier as deception avoidance.

Low Trust or Confidence in Followers.   In chapter 7, we discussed how followers who might be considered out-group members could be characterized as having low trust and confidence placed in them by the manager. The upshot is that when faced with a potential information sharing incident, the manager might be hesitant, believing group members might not respond appropriately to new information (Steele, 1975). The manager might thus feel obliged to keep the information secret with regard to these group members. However, for some people in leadership positions, we see this phenomenon magnifying (i.e., spreading to a larger group of followers) for two key reasons. First, some managers might simply have a difficult time trusting followers, even those that approximate in-group members, with what might be considered sensitive information. Alternatively, they might be acting as "good soldiers" by adhering to the commands of upper management to not share information. That is, the upper echelons might have low level of trust or a lack of confidence in lower level subordinates, and the midlevel manager is simply caught in between in terms of carrying out their orders.

Second, the manager might have an excessive "fear of outliers." So even if his or her out-group is small in number, the manager might not share information with others because of the fear people will talk and such information will get into the hands of the worst of the out-group members. These members will, in turn, use the information in a very destructive manner. As an example, a small group of managers of our academic unit were recently engaged in talks with another unit of the university dealing with the possibility of a merger between the two units. In reality, the other unit was larger and more powerful and desired more of a hostile takeover. In any event, there was fear among the managers that if the nature of these talks was shared with anybody within the university, including people who might be trusted to use the information constructively, the information would somehow end up in the hands of those outliers who might want to cause trouble. For example, they might try to stop such a merger in its tracks or leak the information, or their negative interpretation of the information, to local media. The upshot is no information at all was shared with the broader group, although such sharing could have been used constructively by many group members. If information had been shared openly by those at the top, it is less likely that outliers could distort it destructively. Often information can only be distorted destructively when open information has not been shared and rumors abound.

As another example, several years back we were involved in an upward feedback project in a large police agency that also involved conducting an attitudinal survey as part of the data collection effort. With regard to the latter data, the employees reported negative opinions regarding upper management, personnel policies, and the overall culture of the organization. Top management decided not to share the attitudinal results with employees. Their rationale (at least the reasoning provided to us) was that the data would find their way to the local media, which would only report distortions and inappropriate attributions, such as "corrupt" leadership of the agency. Moreover, they feared that the police officers' union would use the data as a weapon in negotiations with management. These top management members also rationalized that the attitudinal data were not the primary purpose of data collection, as they were contained within a broader upward feedback effort directed toward the development of individuals' leadership qualities.

Nevertheless, as is often the case, word got out to the local media regarding the negative attitudinal data, and inevitably the employees became aware of the general results. Again, the upshot was that employees were disappointed and distrustful of management's decision to withhold this information.

Risk and Conflict Aversion.   The practice of leadership can be a somewhat risky business. Decisions and actions people in the positions of leadership take often involve a high degree of risk. However, many people in these positions are risk-aversive. One such action involves the sharing of information.

There can be a variety of reasons why potential managers might be risk- or conflict-aversive, and thus lack the courage to share information. Quite simply, they might fear failure, uncertainty, or conflict (Daft, 2005). If information is not shared, and the concomitant decision making pertaining to information is handled autocratically, managers might reduce uncertainty and believe their decisions will lead to success. On the other hand, the sharing of information can be risky because of the fear of destructive behavior, as outlined in the preceding examples. However, even if such behavior is not contemplated, managers might lack the courage to put information in the hands of followers. What if, based on shared information, conflict erupts among followers who do not agree with the manager's assessment of the information? What if followers recommend a decision that the manager believes is either not in the best interest of the organization, the manager himself or herself, or both? In short, the sharing of information might go beyond a manager's comfort zone (Diller, 1995), and thus it takes a high degree of courage for a manager (or a collection of managers) to freely share information with followers, thus avoiding the mushroom theory.

Can There Be Positive Motivation for the Mushroom Theory?

We think the answer to this question is yes. There can indeed be more positively motivated reasons for a manager to engage in practices suggestive of the mushroom theory. First, when decision-making processes are ongoing, there might be a felt need to not disclose any information until a decision has already been made. Our earlier example of the food processing firm and its talks with a potential buyer are illustrative of this motivation on the part of management. If the talks were made public, the decision-making process could be disrupted and perhaps unexpected or undesired information might be fed into that process.

The manager might also honestly feel he or she is engaging in the servant leadership role by not sharing information, thus buffering subordinates from the burdens and issues being handled by higher level management. In this way, the manager is serving in a paternalistic role, seemingly looking out for the welfare of subordinates. After all, it might be felt that subordinates have enough problems or burdens of their own, and it is management's job to shield or buffer them from the burdens of upper management and its decision making (Katz & Kahn, 1978). Such thinking represents the positive side of a need-to-know mentality. That is, managers might feel that, for their own welfare, subordinates simply do not need to know about various types of information being considered in decision making. Of course, this is obviously a judgment that management would be making for subordinates. Subordinates might not agree with the judgment regarding specific information or decision-making processes being kept secret. Along these lines, Steele (1975) referred to such thinking as the "Great Lie" theory (p. 25), which would suggest that it is management's role to either withhold information or to simply lie to those below them in the system for their own good, as well as the greater good of the organization.

As an example, we recall a conversation with a CEO and a human resources vice president of a firm about whether or not to inform employees who were working in an older office building about the upcoming asbestos removal over a 4-day weekend. After deciding the health effects to employees would be minimal, they agreed there was no need to alarm employees with the information, thereby causing unfounded concerns or even potential lawsuits.

Another example of positive mushrooming came to light when we were interviewing project managers in a research and development lab. They indicated that they believed it was their job to protect the scientists from bureaucratic issues and administrative decisions that did not directly impact them. They further believed that the scientists needed to be able to focus on their research without such worries. The bottom line is that managers need to be honest with themselves about the true motives for mushrooming. Is the true motivation to protect subordinates, or are more self-serving motives at play being disguised as protection or paternalism?

WHEN THE CROPS FAIL: THE DOWNSIDE OF THE MUSHROOM THEORY

As suggested earlier, our metaphor of the mushroom theory can often go awry in terms of the effects of such behavior on followers and the organization. Instead of growing into healthy delicacies, followers might unfortunately turn into poisonous toadstools. Indeed, most authors who address the mushroom theory (perhaps without directly using the term) would seem to agree that its practice is likely to be problematic.

For example, Pfeffer and Veiga (1999) seemed to oppose the mushroom theory when they listed information sharing as a factor key to organizational success. An interesting example they provided pertains to the Springfield ReManufacturing Corporation, a supplier to such firms as General Motors. This firm employed what they termed the principle of "open-book management." In 1986, General Motors cancelled what amounted to 40% of Springfield's business for the coming year. The firm avoided a layoff by providing its employees with information on what had happened and letting them figure out how to grow the company and achieve the type of productivity gains that would make layoffs unnecessary. Over time, Springfield achieved great financial success (e.g., an initial equity investment of $100,000 in 1983 was worth more than $23 million by 1993). Perhaps more interesting, the firm made money on its open-book management philosophy by running seminars on it. Some companies have clearly benefited by not using the mushroom theory.

Tom Peters is perhaps the most ardent enemy of the mushroom theory. He goes so far as to say that "information distortion" and secrecy constitute "management enemy number one." Peters (1987) stated, "an individual without information cannot take responsibility; an individual who is given information cannot help but take responsibility" (p. 609). He recommended sharing information not only throughout the organization, but with customers and vendors as well. Peters is critical of fear of leaks to competitors—something he termed the "phony threat" (p. 611). He suggested it is phony because there is little, if any, evidence this leakage will actually happen. Moreover, determined competitors will find a way to ferret out hidden information or data anyway.

Additional Case Study Evidence

We were curious about the extent of the practice of the mushroom theory, as well as its effects. In a class of 37 MBA students, as a class project, we asked the students to attempt to identify instances of the mushroom theory in their organizations or other organizations with which they were familiar. Specifically, we asked them to identify instances in which they thought the mushroom theory had occurred. We were careful not to bias the students in one direction or another. Thus, we asked that they only identify situations in which information known to management was not shared with lower level employees. No assertion was made a priori that the lack of information sharing would be necessarily a good thing, a bad thing, neither, or both. Furthermore, in an attempt to not have the students focus on information relevant to one particular manager–employee dyad, we further specified the lack of information sharing should pertain to organizational-level issues, rather than information that would only be of interest to a particular employee.

The students wrote up their cases in 10-page reports. They provided background for their cases including type of industry, the nature of the players involved (i.e., mushrooms and mushroom farmers), and an analysis of what occurred. Fifty-seven percent of the cases were based in service-oriented organizations. Several key findings are worth noting. First, 81% of the experiences were reported by the students as being negative, unpleasant, or unproductive. Second, 70% believed that the lack of information sharing was intentional, as opposed to being inadvertent on the part of management. Third, 60% of the cases reported trust in management was negatively affected on the part of organizational members as a result of information secrecy. In addition, we should note that a number of the cases dealt with either merger and acquisition activities or organizational restructurings.

Some interesting quotes from the cases include the following:

- "There were feelings of shock and mistrust because the acquisition seemed to be out-of- the-blue."
- "We felt like we were being kept in the dark and not part of the 'in-group.' Rampant rumors helped to spread fear."
- "Trust ended up being a big issue for those employees who were actually retained. Management did not withhold information, but employees believed they did. Employees felt that management must have known all along."
- "Rumors were there from the start, and then they were confirmed. People were bitter about losing their jobs. We ended up with people leaving, slow productivity for 6 months, and then there was finally business as usual."
- "In my opinion, if you don't know all of the answers, or if you must keep information confidential, it may be better to simply say when new or correct information will be available. Do not confirm or deny rumors!"
- "People may say that they want to know information, but they really would be angry with having all of it laid out in front of them."

Several interesting things stand out in these quotes. First, trust might indeed be damaged by the practice of the mushroom theory. Second, in the absence of information, or when the information provided is fragmented or not trusted, rumors are likely to run rampant. Third, the final quote given would suggest that information sharing might need to be tempered at times, and there could be a silver lining to the use of the mushroom theory. We explore this issue in more depth at the chapter's conclusion.

How Exactly Might Employees and the Organization Suffer?

The problems that can develop from the practice of the mushroom theory can indeed be serious. We propose a number of negative consequences for individuals, as well as the greater organization. In essence, we see the following problems potentially developing: (a) negative employee attitudes and commitment, (b) reverse mushroom theory, and (c) restricted employee development and organizational learning.

Negative Employee Attitudes and Commitment.   We see a number of negative perceptions, attitudes, and outcomes resulting from practices associated with the mushroom theory. First, it is highly likely that negative attributions will accrue on the part of followers toward those in leadership positions. Followers will begin to question the motives of management and whether managers only have their own self-interests in mind. As demonstrated in our previous case studies, an immediate casualty is trust in management. In short, when managers are perceived as less than forthcoming with critical information, employees will tend to not trust their motives or future decisions and initiatives. An additional casualty is likely to be employee organizational commitment, especially affective commitment, or the extent to which the individual is emotionally attached to the organization. As noted by Yukl (2006), when such commitment is lacking, the individual is likely to resist future influence processes on the part of management.

Second, organizational cynicism on the part of employees is liable to grow, further contributing to a lack of trust and commitment. Dean, Brandes, and Dharwadkar (1998) defined organizational cynicism in terms of a belief that the organization lacks integrity, combined with negative affect toward the organization and a tendency toward destructive behaviors toward the organization consistent with such beliefs and affect. We propose that cynicism is likely to develop when employees begin to feel like "mushrooms." As suggested by Dean et al., likely outcomes of cynicism include frustration with and contempt for management, hopelessness, and lack of citizenship behaviors. As mentioned earlier, in our own research, we have even found that cynicism can stifle improvements in leadership performance among supervisors who receive upward feedback as part of a leader development process (Atwater et al., 2000). Reichers, Wanous, and Austin (1997) noted that to keep cynicism to a minimum, management should share information, involve people in decision making, and keep surprising changes to a minimum. We wholeheartedly concur.

Reverse Mushroom Theory.   When management engages in the mushroom theory on a regular basis, it is likely that employees will take cues from them and model such behavior on their own. As a result, employees themselves are liable to reverse the mushroom theory. In other words, they will keep management in the dark, feed them a lot of manure (or nothing at all), and essentially not care about whether management and the greater organization are productive and vibrant.

In a similar vein, Steele (1975) argued that when there is a climate of information secrecy in an organization, employees will be likely to (a) not disagree with superiors, (b) not raise controversial topics or information for discussion, and (c) only present good news, rather than talk about problems that might be brewing. Thus, there will be a push for only "positive thinking" on the part of people in leadership positions, which will discourage the raising of doubts, questions, or data about current plans or strategies. Obviously, such behavior would lead to the exacerbation of problems and a lack of problem solving, as discussed next.

Restricted Employee Development and Organizational Learning.   As already noted, a key reason in many instances for not sharing information is that management does not have enough confidence in employees that they can or will handle the information constructively. Unfortunately, such thinking can become a self-fulfilling prophecy. According to the Pygmalion effect, people will perform better when their managers have high expectations for them and show confidence in them (Eden, 1990). However, when managers do not share information, thereby not demonstrating high expectations and confidence in employees, we should expect restricted employee development and ability to contribute to problem solving.

A simple, yet common, example might help to illustrate. One very common type of information that is often kept secret or not fully disclosed pertains to financial or budgetary matters. Managers may make financially based decisions without sharing such information with followers, thereby basing decisions on personal assumptions, or even biases and self-interests. Aside from the fostering of poor decisions, a negative side effect is that employees do not learn about the financial aspects of the organization, thereby restricting their own ability to solve or prevent problems pertaining to budgetary or other financial matters.

Increasingly, organizations are relying on the involvement of employees in the process of organizational learning. Crossan, Lane, and White (1999) defined organizational learning in terms of a process of change in thought and action, at both the individual and collective or shared levels. It involves the assimilation of new learning (i.e., exploration), as well as effectively using what has already been learned (i.e., exploitation). Furthermore, the effective management of this tension between novelty and continuity is critical for the strategic renewal of firms (March, 1991).

Berson, Nemanich, Waldman, Galvin, and Keller (2006) recently reviewed literature linking leadership with organizational learning. For example, Vera and Crossan (2004) suggested that for learning to be maximized, people in leadership positions should recognize their limitations (e.g., lack of pertinent knowledge) and share the leadership of organizational learning with lower level colleagues. They specifically articulated the practice of information sharing by suggesting that "top level executives who are available and who manage by walking around convey a clear message about the value of others' opinions, [and that] these leaders help create an environment of information sharing" (p. 228). Vera and Crossan further noted that such leaders "steadfastly explain their vision and keep members up to date with important information" (p. 229).

Is There a Silver Lining?

Before proceeding, we want to briefly consider whether there is a silver lining with regard to the mushroom theory. In other words, can the practice of the mushroom theory sometimes result in positive outcomes or at least be considered as acceptable? We propose that sometimes the answer is yes, although the manager must be cautious, metaphorically "walking on eggshells," and considerate of the context when engaging in such practices. For example, we have suggested that in some instances, employees would rather not be privy to information.

In such circumstances, managers can feel comfortable with the old adage, "What they don't know won't hurt them." By not spreading the information, the manager might actually be doing employees a favor in not having to deal with that information and its negative implications. Moreover, often if information is shared, more work might simply be created for employees—work that could be considered the responsibility of management. It is also the case that at times, the probability that an event will occur is low (e.g., a CEO offhandedly saying that he or she is considering stepping down). Why worry everyone unnecessarily until it is clear that there is something to worry about?

CONCLUSIONS

A message should be coming through fairly clearly at this point: When in doubt, just steer clear of practices that might approximate the mushroom theory. In other words, lean toward open communication, rather than information secrecy or spinning. This message is pretty consistent in both the current and the prior chapter. What should also be clear is that the message contrasts somewhat with recommendations earlier in the book when we were dealing specifically with one-on-one performance feedback. When such feedback is the subject of communication, the manager might be better advised to, at times, withhold information or perceptions or share them in an empathetic or indirect way. We attempt to integrate these two seemingly disparate phenomena in our concluding chapter.

In the next chapter, we continue to attempt to find a potential silver lining as we address the dilemma in which managers often find themselves with regard to the sharing of information. As we have suggested here, most circumstances would point toward sharing, rather than concealing, information. At the same time, we recognize the dilemma faced by managers who might feel the need to be less than forthcoming with certain types of information. We consider this fine line that managers need to walk in the next chapter.

TAKEAWAYS

- If time pressures require managers to make quick decisions without time for input, these time pressures need to be clearly communicated.
- The cycle of managers withholding information, and lower level employees distrusting management based on such behavior, can become a vicious circle.
- There are occasions when not sharing information can buffer employees from burdens and issues that higher management should handle on its own.

- Whenever possible, lean toward open communication rather than information secrecy or distortion. To gain trust and commitment, employees should not be treated like mushrooms!

9

Solutions to the Open Communication Dilemma

Deciding When and How to Share Organizational Information

As we have seen, open communication or information sharing is certainly a dilemma for people in leadership positions. On the one hand, leadership experts and theories would suggest openness of communication, or the concomitant sharing of organizational information, are good things. It makes sense to be open with employees for such purposes as the fostering of employee commitment, the lessening of cynicism, enhanced problem solving, and so forth. In addition, the integrity and interpersonal skills that accompany being an open communicator are associated with managerial advancement within and across the organizations in an individual's career, as opposed to derailment in that career (Van Velsor & Leslie, 1995). On the other hand, recalcitrant or untrustworthy subordinates, personal inclinations, pressures from superiors, and so on, might make managers reluctant to give negative feedback, to keep information secret, or to deceive and spin. They might feel inclined to engage in what we referred to in chapter 8 as the practice of the mushroom theory. So what's the solution?

Unfortunately, there is no clear or easy answer. Leadership in general is a challenging role for managers with many constraints or complexities that keep people with potential leadership skills from actually leading. Indeed, Bennis (1989) wrote a book entitled *Why Leaders Can't Lead*. His basic point is that there are a lot of factors in the contextual environment that keep people in leadership roles from actually leading, including being open communicators. We acknowledge many such factors can be present, as well as personal perceptions and inclinations with which managers themselves must deal. With that said, the goal of this chapter is to provide some insights that will help managers navigate the potentially treacherous maze of information sharing. First, we reiterate and clarify factors pertinent to information sharing, as well as the conditions under which more, rather than less, information should be openly shared. In so doing, we offer some specific recommendations for managers to follow. Second, we consider the organizational and programmatic mechanisms that can help ensure that information sharing on the part of managers will be maximized.

GUIDELINES AND CONSIDERATIONS FOR SHARING INFORMATION

As mentioned earlier in this book, sharing information is a risky business. Thus, many managers might naturally choose to not share information, thereby avoiding risks. Our overall recommendation is that when in doubt, managers should take a little risk and just be open with the information to which they are privy. In other words, they should just divulge information to employees. With that said, however, we provide some heuristics here for managers to consider when balancing information sharing versus secrecy. In essence, these guidelines suggest the types of things managers should consider and how to best deal with those considerations to weigh and balance the extent of information sharing. These include (a) the nature of the actual information to be shared; (b) the nature of followers and their capacity to "handle" shared information; (c) the nature of the managers themselves and the extent of their competence to use information in lieu of information sharing with employees; (d) the balance between appeasing superiors, who might want information to be kept secret, versus leading followers; and (e) media type. Our basic recommendation is to share information as soon as feasible, even if there is some minor risk in doing so.

The Nature of the Information to Be Shared

Many managers have a tendency to overestimate the extent to which information really needs to be kept secret. That is, they overestimate the damage that could be done by sharing it, as well as the extent to which followers cannot "handle" information sharing in a constructive manner.

Regarding the former, a common type of information that could be kept secret is organizational restructuring, especially information pertaining to layoffs, transfers, and so forth. The fear is that if information of such a nature, as well as the decision-making processes surrounding it, were made public, bad things would naturally happen. For example, if an organizational restructuring was likely to lead to layoffs or the movement of employees internally, employees might try to sabotage the initiative in some manner.

However, the opposite might actually occur without information sharing: Bad outcomes are likely. Schweiger and DeNisi (1991) showed that in the absence of effective and open communication, the negative effects of mergers and acquisitions seem to get more serious over time. For those whose confidence and trust are already somewhat low, perceptions of uncertainty and stress will be elevated, which only serves to heighten potential resistance to change. The upshot could be hostility among survivors, or the type of emotional withdrawal or voluntary turnover behavior on the part of managers at the acquired firm that is often documented in the merger and acquisition literature (Light, 2001; Lubatkin, Schweiger, & Weber, 1999).

We are not suggesting that information should never be kept secret. There could be circumstances, legal or otherwise, in which certain types of information must be held close to the vest, at least for some period of time. On the other hand, we are also suggesting here that managers might have a tendency to overestimate those circumstances and the length of time information needs to be kept secret. Our advice is to think carefully about how soon information can be shared, rather than how long it can be kept quiet.

The Nature of Followers

Intertwined with concerns about the nature of information, managers might have concerns about the nature of followers and their ability to deal with information effectively and constructively. Two concerns could be present here. First, managers might not feel that followers have the ability to understand or deal with information (e.g., through involvement in decision making). Second, and probably more important, managers might feel followers lack the commitment to organizational goals, and thus would not handle the sharing of information in a constructive manner (Vroom, 2000; Vroom & Jago, 1995).

If we dissect these concerns, it becomes evident in many circumstances that the perceived problem lies with a minority (i.e., sometimes a very small number) of employees. However, because there might be a fear of leakage to that minority, information is not shared with the vast majority of people who have both the ability and commitment to use or deal with the information constructively. Our contention is that for the benefit of the majority and the overall organization, managers should generally take the risk and share information, which would probably also entail more involvement in the decision making that often accompanies shared information.

A question to ask is how much damage could possibly be done by a few likely low-credibility employees, versus the damage to trust and morale across the organization.

The Nature of the Managers

As we have seen, information sharing and decision making are intertwined roles for managers. A key reason for either sharing information, or conversely not sharing information, is that it is interwoven into managerial decision-making processes. Thus, if a manager decides to be more participative in that process, it will inevitably mean that more information will be shared. After all, people cannot be effectively involved in the process if they do not have relevant information. Moreover, the mere fact that there is participation could mean management is "letting the cat out of the bag" in terms of sharing information. That is, the problem to be decided, in and of itself, represents information. Such problems could include a potential restructuring, a change in work procedures, and so forth.

On the other hand, when little or no participation is allowed with regard to decision making, the information represented in the problem being considered will more naturally be kept secret. Thus, there will be a tendency to invoke the "the need to know" principle. Because the manager will have already taken the first step of more autocratic decision-making style, it is natural to take the next step of keeping the problem and its consideration secret. Secrecy will then be maintained until the decision and its ramifications are announced. At that point, it is quite likely that subordinates will perceive being treated like mushrooms with all of the negative outcomes discussed in chapter 8.

Case Example

A business manager did not believe that it was appropriate to share information about the budget with department heads or employees, even though it had been requested numerous times. The rationale was that if the department heads learned that there were discretionary funds at his disposal, they would pester him for it. A new manager was brought in who showed complete transparency with the budget, both in terms of what was available, as well as expenses. It was clear from this level of communication that the company's revenue was not keeping up with expenditures and within a few years there would be no more discretionary funds if either revenue or expenditures did not change. Department heads and employees were motivated to increase revenue and decrease spending. In part, it was a case of trust and confidence in followers.

DEALING WITH PERCEPTIONS OF THE CONTEXT, FOLLOWERS, AND ONESELF

Why would a manager keep information secret and make autocratic decisions when he or she could have chosen an alternative process that would have been more open in terms of communication? The first part of this question is obviously complex with no simple explanations. Managers show autocratic behavior for a number of reasons. For example, they might work in organizational contexts in which showing such leadership is the norm, and even expected. Moreover, they might believe the role of managers is to make decisions, whereas the role of subordinates is to implement those decisions. Although there is no doubt that decision making is a key role associated with management (Yukl, 2006), the precise manner or process by which decisions are made can vary, and can certainly include participation or input on the part of followers.

A further explanation can be found in the perceptions of managers regarding followers, as well as themselves. If we examine Vroom and Jago's (1988) model of contingency leadership, it is clear that managers are expected to estimate two types of commitment on the part of followers: (a) the extent to which subordinates are committed to carrying out a decision, especially if the decision was made without their involvement; and (b) the extent to which subordinates have commitment to the organization's goals. In addition, managers are expected to estimate the competence of subordinates to effectively contribute to a decision-making process.

We contend that managers will tend to overestimate the extent to which decisions made autocratically will be supported and carried out by followers. In many contexts, employee commitment cannot be guaranteed, and indeed, decisions can even be undermined. For example, contexts involving knowledge workers are especially prone to such issues pertaining to the need for employee commitment. Employees might spend a good deal of time and energy figuring out how to get around a decision rather than abiding by it. In the flex-time example provided in an earlier chapter, employees could begin to use sick and vacation days on alternate Fridays to resume some of their previously flexible hours.

In addition, we suggest that managers are likely to underestimate both subordinate commitment to organizational goals, as well as their competence and expertise to contribute to a decision-making process. In the flex-time case, employees might have had knowledge and ideas about alternative ways to schedule work. If managers fail to share information about an impending decision with followers, not only will pertinent information not be brought to bear on the problem, but the perceived lack of subordinate commitment to organizational goals could become a self-fulfilling prophecy. That is, by being treated as a "mushroom," and concomitantly by not being involved in decision making, subordinates are likely to have reduced commitment to organizational goals. Self-fulfilling prophecies can work in both positive and negative directions.

To summarize, managers evaluate subordinates either implicitly or explicitly when it comes time to make decisions, and to share, versus not share, information. Our contention is that managers could be prone to misjudgment, which would lend itself to more autocratic decision making and less sharing of information. We caution managers to more carefully consider these judgments and to orient themselves toward the developmental mode stressed by Vroom and Jago (1988), as well as by other leadership theorists (e.g., Bass, 1990a, 1997). By doing so, there will ultimately be more of a tendency to openly communicate.

We should also recognize that managers evaluate themselves in decision-making processes. Specifically, they evaluate the personal level of knowledge or expertise that they can bring to bear in solving a problem or making a decision. Unfortunately, such an evaluation is often wrong and in the direction of overrating. That is, managers might overestimate the extent of their knowledge or expertise as it pertains to problem solving. In so doing, they will have a tendency toward making decisions on their own, which, as already noted, goes along with keeping information regarding the problem being considered close to the vest. However, research has demonstrated performance problems for managers who tend to overrate themselves in relation to how others view them (Atwater & Yammarino, 1992; Yammarino & Atwater, 1993). Along similar lines, we contend that managers who overestimate their own personal knowledge or expertise with regard to decision making are likely to achieve negative outcomes in terms of poor decision quality, lack of employee commitment, and so forth.

In simple terms, what is necessary on the part of managers is a degree of humility in their own self-concept. Collins (2001) referred to the "Level 5 leader" as one who channels his or her ego and ambition into building a great organization. He or she is humble at the personal level but extremely ambitious at the organizational level. Furthermore, such leaders do not overestimate their own expertise. "The good-to-great leaders never wanted to become larger-than-life heroes. They never aspired to be put on a pedestal or become unreachable icons. They were seemingly ordinary people quietly producing extraordinary results" (Collins, 2001, p. 28). In contrast, more narcissistic leaders (Maccoby, 2004) are likely to follow the "Genius with a thousand helpers" (Collins, 2001, p. 45) model, where the leader possesses grandiose ideas, does not share information with subordinates (or even is deceptive with regard to information), makes decisions autocratically, and designates others to simply implement those decisions.

WALKING THE TIGHTROPE BETWEEN
LEADING FOLLOWERS AND APPEASING SUPERIORS

To this point, we have considered effective leadership and the role that open communication plays. We have assumed that managers are the masters of their own fates, and if they choose, they can be more open communicators. However, it is also important to recognize that they exist within a context. Much of that context we consider later in this chapter as we look at system-level factors that can help set the stage for, or enable, open communication in organizations. Here, we examine the fact that except for the top executive in an organization, managers are in follower roles, as well as leader roles.

Effective followership involves building a positive relationship with one's manager, as well as being a resource to the manager and helping him or her to be a better manager. For example, the manager is likely to value loyalty and followers who help him or her accomplish organizational goals. With that said, it is not all about being a "yes-man" and doing whatever the manager says or deems appropriate. Part of being a good follower involves what Kelley (1992) referred to as critical, independent thinking. A follower who includes such behavior in his or her role will, when appropriate, offer constructive criticism and not "sacrifice their personal integrity for the good of the organization in order to maintain harmony" (Daft, 2005, p. 263). In reality, effective managers will want subordinates who challenge them. Sager and Brady (1999) pointed to the case example of how Lou Gerstner (former CEO of IBM) hired Larry Ricciardi to be senior vice president and corporate counsel, despite the fact he knew Ricciardi would challenge his decisions and his thinking.

What does all of this have to do with information sharing and treading the balance between being a leader and being a good follower? There are likely to be times when a manager seeking to practice effective leadership will prefer to share information and decision-making processes with followers. However, his or her manager will ask, or even insist, that lower level subordinates not be in the information loop, at least not until decisions have been made and a course of action established. We acknowledge such a situation presents a difficult conundrum for the manager who is caught in the middle. Nevertheless, as noted earlier, effective leadership involves integrity, and effective followership involves constructively challenging upper level management when the circumstances would seem to dictate its appropriateness. Thus, both leadership and followership principles would seem to suggest the manager-in-the-middle should not just blindly or dutifully accept the desires of upper management.

We see two choices. First, the manager can simply confront upper level individuals and lobby for information sharing based on principles that we have articulated in this book. Second, if the first option did not work, the manager could choose to leave or withdraw from the situation, rather than sacrificing his or her integrity. This latter option is obviously more drastic. However, if the nature of the information and associated decisions are important enough, such a choice might seem unavoidable.

MEDIA TYPE

It would be remiss to consider any form or style of communication, including the sharing of information or open communication, without also considering media type. These days communication can occur through a variety of media including e-mail or teleconferencing, as well as traditional face-to-face and telephone conversations. Indeed, more technologically advanced media (e.g., e-mail) are often useful for communicating routine messages and announcements. However, the issues surrounding the type of information we have considered in this section of the book are often quite sensitive in nature, involving potential stress and related emotional reactions on the part of organizational members. People often come across as lacking sensitivity, distant, and even arrogant when attempting to communicate such delicate issues through media such as e-mail (Hallowell, 1999; Poe, 2003).

We have observed instances of high-level managers not revealing information, nor allowing participation in decision-making processes pertaining to information. Further, we have seen such behavior combined with the use of e-mail or other printed announcements (e.g., newspaper columns) in which lower level organizational members were informed at a late date about controversial information, as well as the outcomes of decisions relevant to that information. Thus, it became clear that relevant information and decision-making processes had been kept secret. The effect was a high degree of employee outrage and disillusionment with management.

It is likely that managers knew such a lack of information sharing and involvement in decision making would be received in a less-than-friendly manner, and thus were hesitant to share it in a public, face-to-face forum. Nevertheless, we caution that the use of e-mail or other print media can have negative employee outcomes, especially when the sharing of information represents more of an after-the-fact announcement. If a manager feels that he or she must engage in mushroom theory practices, then he or she is at least beholding to have the courage to address employees in a face-to-face manner when the information and accompanying decision are finally shared.

ORGANIZATIONAL AND PROGRAMMATIC RECOMMENDATIONS

We have emphasized the act of being a more open communicator is largely in the hands of the individual leader. If the leader shows confidence in followers, shows some degree of humility in his or her own capabilities or knowledge, and manages his or her boss correctly, the leader should be able to be a more open communicator with regard to information to which followers will want to be privy. By being a more open communicator, the leader stands less of a chance of being perceived as engaging in the mushroom theory of leadership, as described in the previous chapter.

At the same time, we acknowledge that leaders do not exist in a vacuum, and they are highly susceptible to organizational or system-level factors that can influence their behaviors and actions. In the remainder of this chapter, we examine such factors with the hope of giving guidance to organizations seeking to be more open in their communication, thereby maximizing such outcomes as employee commitment, identification, and creativity. We consider selection, reward, and development mechanisms for managers.

Selecting Open Communicators

Numerous techniques exist for the selection or placement of managers, including interviews, an examination of one's experiences, and even paper-and-pencil testing. It is beyond the scope of this book to review all of these options. However, a few possibilities seem especially relevant for screening individuals who might be more prone toward being open communicators, rather than "mushroom farmers."

First, behavioral interviewing has grown in popularity over time as a way to better understand tendencies of prospective managers in specific types of situations (e.g., Clifford, 2006). In a behavioral interview, a candidate could be asked to think about a time or a situation in his or her past where that individual might have faced the dilemma of sharing critical information with subordinates, versus keeping such information secret. Specifics could be probed, such as what exactly the candidate did and felt (e.g., "What were you thinking at that point" or "Lead me through your decision-making process in that instance"), how the candidate evaluated follower ability to effectively handle the information, the potential dilemma of dealing with a superior who did not want to have the information shared, and so forth. In short, the goal would be to use the data produced by a behavioral interview to evaluate the candidate's potential for being an effective, open communicator.

Second, instead of trying to get the candidate to replay past behaviors, simulation techniques could be used to see how the individual deals with open communication scenarios in the present. In general, the use of simulation techniques to select and develop managerial talent has shown much promise over time (Thornton & Cleveland, 1990). More specifically, assessment center techniques have been used for such purposes with much success (Howard & Bray, 1988; Waldman & Korbar, 2004). Although we are not aware of specific applications, we can envision how assessment center techniques might be used to identify the potential for open communication practices as a leader.

For example, simulated interview and leaderless group discussion formats could be used to see how prospective leaders might deal with the sharing of information. The scenario presented in chapter 1 in which the owners of a natural foods company had spent time in private meetings with a potential purchaser of the company would seem ripe for either format. In a simulated interview, a trained interviewer could present the scenario and then probe the interviewee as to how he or she might deal with the potential sharing of information. Would the interviewee attempt to deceive members of the organization with regard to the possible purchase of the organization (i.e., "feed them a lot of manure")? Would he or she attempt to be more open about the potential purchase, or point the conversation in a positive direction without directly mentioning the acquisition negotiations (e.g., by suggesting that eventually the firm will need to be sold, and that perhaps employees should organize themselves for the possibility of purchasing it)? Similarly, such an open communications problem or dilemma could be presented in a leaderless group discussion format in which various members of the group could be assessed on the degree to which they encouraged and supported more open communication, versus deception or information secrecy. In sum, we see assessment center methods as a viable possibility for the selection of leaders with open communication skills or tendencies.

Appraisal and Reward Mechanisms

For years, agency theorists have suggested that for managers to be good agents of the firm, their actions and decisions must be tightly controlled in terms of appraisal and reward mechanisms (Jensen, 2001; Jensen & Meckling, 1976). Specifically, they should be geared toward the singular pursuit of value or profit maximization. In addition, management gurus have stressed the importance of relatively simple performance metrics when dealing with the accomplishment of objectives (e.g., Blanchard & Johnson, 1982). Thus, it should not be surprising that managers are appraised and rewarded largely on the basis of performance objectives and outcomes. So where might effectiveness in the role of being an open communicator fit into appraisal and reward mechanisms?

We see two developments that would suggest that being an open communicator can (and should) be considered in the mix of the appraisal and rewarding of effective managers. First, as mentioned earlier, the integrity and interpersonal skills that accompany being an open communicator are associated with managerial advancement, as opposed to derailment (Van Velsor & Leslie, 1995). Those managers who are perceived by others to be reluctant to share decision making, to be resistant to input from others, to devalue others' contributions, and to order people around are far more likely to see their careers derail (fail to advance beyond midlevel positions) than managers who do not engage in these behaviors. Thus, open communication tendencies might have long-term reward benefits for leaders. Second, open communication in this section of the book is largely akin to aspects of transformational leadership, and meta-analyses have shown such forms of leadership to have consistent relationships with motivational and performance outcomes on the part of the followers and the organizations being led (Judge & Piccolo, 2004; Lowe et al., 1996). In short, it would seem that managers should be appraised and rewarded, at least in part, on the extent to which they show transformational leadership and open communication behavior.

With that said, the conundrum faced by organizations is that appraisal and reward systems are controlled at higher levels of management, whereas the experience and effective appraisal of leadership rests with followers. Thus, it is relatively straightforward for one's boss to appraise the extent to which quantifiable performance goals are reached. On the other hand, it is more difficult for one's boss to assess leadership, as the primary recipients of leadership are one's subordinates.

A potential solution is the incorporation of multisource feedback procedures into appraisal and reward systems, whereby followers are asked to assess the extent to which a manager is an open communicator, as opposed to being a "mushroom farmer." Unfortunately, when multisource feedback processes are used for evaluative rather than developmental purposes, there can be some negative side effects (Atwater, Waldman, & Brett, 2002; Waldman, Atwater, & Antonioni, 1998). For example, game playing with regard to ratings could occur. Specifically, managers might make implicit or explicit deals with followers to give them high upward feedback ratings in exchange for high performance appraisal ratings of the followers at a later point in time. In noting this problem, Waldman and Atwater (2001) also suggested that if multisource feedback processes are repeated over time with no evaluative consequences, raters of individuals who repeatedly receive poor scores are liable to get frustrated with the process. Further, they might "perhaps discontinue their input, if it appears that no changes are being made and their ratings are put to no evaluative use" (Waldman & Atwater, 2001, p. 469). The upshot is that despite the potential negative side effects of making multisource feedback processes somewhat evaluative, they nevertheless represent a mechanism for appraising and rewarding open communication behavior.

Developing Open Communicators

We envision at least three possible approaches to the development of open communication skills and behaviors on the part of managers, and each of the approaches would rely on feedback as a means of clarifying one's behaviors or tendencies. First, instead of being used for selection, assessment centers have increasingly been used for developmental purposes (Guthrie & Kelly-Radford, 1998; Munchus & McArthur,

1991). The idea is to provide participants with intensive, developmental feedback on performance-based dimensions, which could include something akin to open communication skills.

Second, multisource feedback programs have been used much more frequently for development, rather than evaluative purposes (Waldman & Atwater, 2001; Waldman et al., 1998). It is possible to have items in such surveys specifically targeted toward open communication practices on the positive side, or deception and spinning on the more negative side. Feedback could then be provided in a report. However, to receive maximum developmental benefit, it is best to couple the feedback report with some sort of facilitation, either in a group or workshop setting (Seifert, Yukl, & McDonald, 2003) or one-on-one between participant and facilitator (Chappelow, 1998). Furthermore, improvements are more likely if managers hold follow-up meetings with subordinates to discuss the feedback received from them (Walker & Smither, 1999). Such a meeting can help clarify why a manager might be rated relatively low in terms of open communication, and it could increase the manager's sense of accountability to use the feedback to make improvements in his or her behavior (Yukl, 2006).

Third, we suggest executive coaching could be a means for developing open communication skills and tendencies on the part of managers. Such coaching has become an increasingly popular mechanism for developing leaders in organizations (Hall, Otazo, & Hollenbeck, 1999). The coach could be used to provide advice and feedback about how to handle specific challenges, such as dealing with a current situation involving potential open communication versus information secrecy. Thus, the coach can help evaluate the context, followers, expertise of the leader, and potential conflicts with the boss. Effective coaches provide honest and accurate feedback, as well as clear and relevant advice (Dotlich & Cairo, 1999). Moreover, executive coaching could be used in conjunction with techniques already mentioned, such as multisource feedback. In sum, coaching offers particular advantages over other forms of development, including convenience and the providing of personal attention.

CONCLUSIONS

Open communication can represent a dilemma for managers. On the one hand, when it comes to information to which subordinates might like to be privy, leadership theory and just plain common sense would suggest managers should strive to be more open communicators. In so doing, they will avoid being the "mushroom farmers" described in the previous chapter. In addition, as we have seen, open communication and participative decision making tend to go hand in hand. So out of necessity, the manager is likely to be more of an open communicator to simultaneously be more involving with subordinates. On the other hand, there can be circumstances that would seemingly prevent managers from being open communicators. As we have seen, these circumstances include aspects of the information to be shared, aspects of the followers and managers themselves, and pressures from the boss.

In this chapter, we have considered these circumstances. We have also attempted to provide specific advice and solutions for managers as they consider their own open communication skills and tendencies. Furthermore, we have suggested organizational or programmatic remedies that would be applicable to systems involving groups of managers. As with other aspects of effective leadership, the challenges are great, but so are the rewards for individuals and organizations that are able to realize more effective open communication.

TAKEAWAYS

- In the absence of effective and open communication, the negative effects of mergers and acquisitions seem to get more serious over time.
- For the benefit of the majority of employees, and the overall organization, managers should generally take the risk and share more information.
- Managers need to weigh the risk of information sharing against the risks of making a decision with inadequate or faulty information.
- Managers tend to overestimate the extent to which decisions made autocratically will be supported and carried out by followers.
- Managers are likely to underestimate both employee commitment to the organization's goals and their competence and expertise to contribute to the decision-making process.
- If a manager feels he or she must withhold information, he or she should have the courage to address employees face to face when the information and accompanying decision are finally shared.
- Selection techniques such as behavioral interviewing and simulations can be used to help select managers who are likely to be open communicators.
- Executive coaching could be a means for developing open communication skills.

10

Putting It All Together

We have examined the topic of open communication in this book, and how people in leadership positions are faced with two critical dilemmas when engaging in such behavior. First, there is the challenge of being open as communicator when delivering one-on-one performance feedback to an individual, often in the context of a manager–subordinate relationship. Norms and common sense might suggest that a manager should be as open as possible, but as we have seen, such openness can actually be very problematic at times. Second, there is the challenge of being an open communicator when delivering information to individuals, groups, and even the greater organization regarding occurrences, changes of policy or structure, and so forth. The type of information that we considered in chapters 7 through 9 does not pertain to individuals' performance, but rather to issues and events of an organizational nature for which members might have a felt need to know.

Although the information contained within these two challenges are different in nature, in their own ways, they each pose dilemmas for managers attempting to engage effectively in their leadership role. In each case, the dilemma pertains to the level of openness for which the manager should strive in his or her communication. We have overviewed the issues surrounding these dilemmas including the nature of managers, followers, organizations, and the information itself. As we put things together in this concluding chapter, we summarize how these communication dilemmas differ, as well as share similarities.

DIFFERENCES IN OUR COMMUNICATION DILEMMAS

The first communication dilemma regarding face-to-face feedback is probably the most common problem faced by managers. It can occur on a day-to-day basis or at formal times of appraisal. The second dilemma, open communication about organizational issues, might not be as frequent, but its importance can be immense with regard to manager–follower relationships, employee commitment, and so forth. Indeed, as shown by the examples in chapters 7 through 9, the inadequate handling of information pertaining to organizational phenomena can lead to followers feeling like proverbial "mushrooms," which can in turn lead to some problematic outcomes.

These communication dilemmas also differ in their level of analysis. That is, one-on-one performance feedback is at the individual level of analysis. Conversely, the second dilemma previously mentioned is more typically at the group or organizational level. In other words, it pertains to information emanating from organizational phenomena that, in turn, is communicated at the group or organizational levels. In sum, the dilemma of being an open communicator is not limited to the individual level of analysis. Instead, we have shown that it has implications for broader group- or organizational-level issues.

SIMILARITIES IN OUR COMMUNICATION DILEMMAS

Despite these differences, there are also similarities concerning the open communication dilemmas that we have identified. First, dealing with these dilemmas could require defying what might seem to be common sense, but in different ways. Specifically, it might seem like common sense to be more of an open communicator when it comes to one-on-one performance feedback with followers. However, as we have seen, such open communication can actually be detrimental when the feedback is negative in nature and when it is delivered poorly or the receiver cannot handle it. Conversely, it might seem like common sense to many managers that one should be extremely cautious in sharing information with followers regarding such organizational issues or occurrences as restructuring, potential policy changes, and so forth. However, again as we have shown, leadership theory and research would seem to point toward erring in the direction of more openness and sharing, rather than less. The bottom line is that, as is the case with other managerial phenomena, there is more than meets the eye with regard to the dilemma of open communication. Managers seeking to effectively practice their leadership role should be cautious about blindly engaging in behavior that would seem to be in line with common sense.

Second, for both types of communication dilemmas, there can be positive outcomes. When being a more open communicator with regard to one-on-one performance feedback, the manager can clearly communicate perceptions and expectations without holding back. The upside is that followers will clearly understand the manager and the implications for them as organizational members. Regarding the communication of organizational information, followers will feel more engaged and trusted as a result of open communication, which, in turn, should lead to positive outcomes in terms of their motivation and commitment, as well as problem solving.

Third, it is important to be aware that open communication can engender negative consequences for both types of communication dilemmas. The potential negative outcomes associated with open one-on-one performance feedback can include such things as deteriorated manager–follower relationships and withdrawal on the part of followers. The open communication of organizational information can lead to such problems as leakage to the media or competitors and raising fears and stress levels among followers, which might not need to be raised.

CONCLUDING STATEMENT

So, where does this all leave us? Our goal in this book has been to provide information relevant to the two communication dilemmas addressed here. Specifically, we have considered these communication dilemmas, relevant theory and research, and potential solutions. Armed with such information, managers are in a better position to more adequately deal with the challenges posed by open communication in attempting to maximize the advantages or positive outcomes and minimize the negative outcomes. We hope our discussions, case examples, and takeaways leave readers with a better sense of what to communicate, and how, when, and why open communication should be practiced.

However, as with other challenges pertaining to the leadership role, there is no magic bullet. The effective practice of leadership requires careful consideration of the types of issues presented in this book in a lifelong attempt to develop ourselves as better managers. Our hope is that we have been able to provide some insights that will help foster better leadership practice.

References

Adler, N. J. (1980). Cultural synergy: The management of cross-cultural organizations. In W. W. Burke & L. D. Goodstein (Eds.), *Trends and issues in OD: Current theory and practice* (pp. 163–184). San Diego, CA: University Associates.

Adler, N. J. (2002). *International dimensions of organizational behavior* (4th ed.). Cincinnati, OH: South-Western College Publishing.

Adler, N. J., Doktor, R., & Redding, S. G. (1986). From the Atlantic to the Pacific Century: Cross-cultural management reviewed. *Journal of Management, 12,* 295–318.

Alloy, L. B., & Ahrens, A. H. (1987). Depression and pessimism for the future: Biased use of statistically relevant information in predictions for self versus others. *Journal of Personality and Social Psychology, 52,* 366–378.

Andersen, P. (1991). Explaining intercultural differences in nonverbal communication as cited in Weaver, R. (1993). *Understanding Interpersonal Communication* (6th ed.), 292. Harper Collins: NY.

Arvey, R. D., & Jones, A. P. (1985). The use of discipline in organizational settings: A framework for future research. *Research in Organizational Behavior, 7,* 367–408.

Ashford, S. J. (1986). The feedback environment: An exploratory study of cue use. *Journal of Organizational Behavior, 14,* 201–224.

Ashford, S. J. (1988). Individual strategies for coping with stress during organizational transitions. *Journal of Applied Behavioral Science, 24,* 19–36.

Ashford, S., & Tsui, A. (1991). Self-regulation for managerial effectiveness: The role of active feedback seeking. *Academy of Management Journal, 34,* 251–280.

Atkinson, J. W. (1964). *An introduction to motivation.* Princeton, NJ: Van Nostrand.

Atkinson, J. W. (1974). The mainsprings of achievement-oriented activity. In J. W. Atkinson & J. O. Raynor (Eds.), *Motivation and achievement* (pp. 13–41). New York: Wiley.

Atwater, L. E., & Brett, J. F. (2005). Antecedents and consequences of reactions to developmental 360 degree feedback. *Journal of Vocational Behavior, 66,* 532–548.

Atwater, L. E., & Brett, J. F. (in press). Feedback format: Does it influence managers' reactions to feedback? *Journal of Occupational and Organizational Psychology.*

Atwater, L., Brett, J., Waldman, D., DiMare, L., & Hayden, M. (2003). Male and female perceptions of the gender-typing of management sub-roles. *Sex Roles, 50,* 191–199.

Atwater, L. E., Carey, J., & Waldman, D. A. (2001). Gender and discipline in the workplace: Wait until your father gets home. *Journal of Management, 27,* 537–561.

Atwater, L. E., Goldman, A., & Charles, A. (2006). *Interactional justice and discipline delivery: The importance of explanations.* Paper presented at the annual meeting of the Society for Industrial and Organizational Psychology, Dallas, TX. April.

Atwater, L. E., Waldman, D. A., Atwater, D., & Cartier, P. (2000). An upward feedback field experiment: Supervisors' cynicism, follow-up, and commitment to subordinates. *Personnel Psychology, 53,* 275–297.

Atwater, L. E., Waldman, D. A., & Brett, J. F. (2002). Understanding and optimizing multisource feedback. *Human Resource Management, 41,* 193–208.

Atwater, L. E., Waldman, D. A., Carey, J. A., & Cartier, P. (2001). Recipient and observer reactions to discipline: Are managers experiencing wishful thinking? *Journal of Organizational Behavior, 22,* 249–270.

Atwater, L., & Yammarino, F. (1992). Does self–other agreement on leadership perceptions moderate the validity of leadership and performance predictions? *Personnel Psychology, 45,* 141–164.

Avolio, B. J., Gardner, W. L., Walumbwa, F. O., Luthans, F., & May, D. R. (2004). Unlocking the mask: A look at the process by which authentic leaders impact follower attitudes and behavior. *The Leadership Quarterly, 15,* 801–823.

Bailey, J. R., Chen, C. C., & Dou, S. (1997). Conceptions of self and performance-related feedback in the United States, Japan and China. *Journal of International Business Studies, 28,* 605–625.

Bandura, A. (1986). *Social foundations of thought and action.* Englewood Cliffs, NJ: Prentice-Hall.

Bandura, A. (1991). Social cognitive theory of self-regulation. *Organizational Behavior and Human Decision Processes, 50,* 248–287.

Bandura, A., & Cervone, D. (1983). Self-evaluative and self-efficacy mechanisms governing the motivational effects of goal systems. *Journal of Personality and Social Psychology, 45,* 1017–1028.

Baron, R. A. (1988). Negative effects of destructive criticism: Impact on conflict, self-efficacy, and task performance. *Journal of Applied Psychology, 73,* 199–207.

Baron, R. A. (1990). Countering the effects of destructive criticism: The relative efficacy of four interventions. *Journal of Applied Psychology, 75,* 235–245.

Baron, R. A. (1996). "La vie en rose" revisited: Contrasting perceptions of informal upward feedback among managers and subordinates. *Management Communication Quarterly, 9,* 338–348.

Bass, B. M. (1990a). *Bass & Stogdill's handbook of leadership: Theory, research, and managerial applications* (3rd ed.). New York: Free Press.

Bass, B. M. (1990b). From transactional to transformational leadership: Learning to share the vision. *Organizational Dynamics, 18*(3), 19–31.

Bass, B. M. (1997). Does the transactional-transformational leadership paradigm transcend organizational and national boundaries? *American Psychologist, 52,* 130–139.

Bass, B. M., & Avolio, B. J. (1993). Transformational leadership: A response to critiques. In M. M. Chemers & R. Ayman (Eds.), Leadership theory and research: Perspectives and directions (pp. 49–80). San Diego, CA: Academic.

Bass, B. M., & Steidlmeier, P. (1999). Ethics, character, and authentic transformational leadership behavior. The Leadership Quarterly, 10, 181–217.

Baumeister, R., & Jones, E. E. (1978). When self-presentation is constrained by the target's knowledge: Consistency and compensation. *Journal of Personality and Social Psychology, 36,* 608–618.

Beebe, S., & Masterson, J. (1990). Communicating in small groups: Principles and practices. 3rd ed. Glenview, IL: Scott Foresman.

Benedict, M. E., & Levine, E. L. (1988). Delay and distortion: Tacit influences on performance appraisal effectiveness. *Journal of Applied Psychology, 73,* 507–514.

Bennis, W. (1989). *Why leaders can't lead: The unconscious conspiracy continues.* San Francisco: Jossey-Bass.

Berson, Y., Nemanich, L., Waldman, D. A., Galvin, B., & Keller, R. (2006). Leadership and organizational learning: A multiple levels perspective. *The Leadership Quarterly, 17,* 6, 577–594.

Birdwhistell, R. (1970). *Kinesics and context: Essays on body motion communication.* Philadelphia: University of Pennsylvania Press.

Blanchard, K., & Johnson, S. (1982). *The one-minute manager.* New York: Morrow.

Block, P. (1993). *Stewardship: Choosing service over self-interest.* San Francisco: Berrett-Koehler.

Boddy, J., Carver, A., & Rowley, K. (1986). Effects of positive and negative verbal reinforcement on performance as a function of extraversion-introversion: Some tests of Gray's theory. *Personality and Individual Differences, 7,* 81–88.

Boehm, V. R. (1968). Mr. Prejudice, Miss Sympathy, and the authoritarian personality: An application of psychological measuring techniques to the problem of jury selection. *Wisconsin Law Review, 43,* 734.

Bond, M., Wan, K., Leung, K., & Giacalone, R. (1985). How are responses to verbal insults related to cultural collectivism and power distance? *Journal of Cross-Cultural Psychology, 16,* 11–127.

Bracken, D. W. (1996). *Multisource (360 degree) feedback: Surveys for individual and organizational development.* San Francisco: Jossey-Bass.

Bracken, D., Timmreck, C., & Church, A. (2001). *The handbook of multisource feedback.* San Francisco: Jossey-Bass.

Brenner, O. C., Tomkiewicz, J., & Schein, V. E. (1989). The relationship between sex role stereotypes and requisite management characteristics revisited. *Academy of Management Review, 14,* 661–669.

Brett, J. F., & Atwater, L. E. (2001). 360-degree feedback: Perceptions of accuracy, reactions, and perceptions of usefulness. *Journal of Applied Psychology, 86,* 930–942.

Brett, J. F., Atwater, L. E., & Waldman, D. A. (2005). Effective delivery of workplace discipline: Do women have to be more participatory than men? *Group and Organization Management, 30,* 487–513.

Brown, J. D. (1986). Evaluations of self and others: Self-enhancement biases in social judgments. *Social Cognition, 4,* 353–376.

Buck, R. (1984). *The communication of emotion.* New York: Guilford Press.

Burke, R., Weitzel, W., & Weir, T. (1978). Characteristics of effective employee performance review and development interviews: Replication and extension. *Personnel Psychology, 31,* 903–919.

Butler, J., & Cantrell, R. (1984). A behavioral decision theory approach to modeling dyadic trust in superiors and subordinates. *Psychological Reports, 55,* 19–28.

Campion, M. A., & Lord, R. G. (1982). A control systems conceptualization of goal setting process. *Organizational Behavior and Human Performance, 30,* 265–287.

Carothers, B. J., & Allen, J. B. (1999). Relationships of employment status, gender role, insult, and gender with use of influence tactics. *Sex Roles, 41,* 516.

Cederblom, D. (1982). The performance appraisal interview: A review, implications, and suggestions. *Academy of Management Review, 7,* 219–227.

Chappelow, C. T. (1998). 360-degree feedback. In C. D. McCauley, R. S. Moxley, & E. Van Velsor (Eds.), *Center for Creative Leadership handbook of leadership development* (pp. 29–65). San Francisco: Jossey-Bass.

Charles, A., Atwater, L., & Goldman, A. (2007). *Interactional justice and discipline delivery: The importance of explanations.* Working paper. Arizona State University.

Chaney, L., & Martin, J. (1995). *Intercultural business communication.* Upper Saddle River, NJ: Prentice-Hall.

Choi, Y., & Mai-Dalton, R. R. (1998). On the leadership function of self-sacrifice. *The Leadership Quarterly, 9,* 475–501.

Chung, Y. B., Marshall, J. A., & Gordon, L. L. (2001). Racial and gender biases in supervisory evaluation and feedback. *Clinical Supervisor, 20,* 99–111.

Clifford, S. (2006). The new science of hiring. *Business Week, 28*(8), 90–98.

Collins, J. C. (2001). *Good to great.* New York: Harper Business.

Conger, J. A. (1990). The dark side of leadership. *Organizational Dynamics, 19*(2), 44–55.

Cotton, J. L., Vollrath, D. A., Froggatt, K. L., Lengnick-Hall, M. L., & Jennings, K. R. (1988). Employee participation: Diverse forms and different outcomes. *Academy of Management Review, 13,* 8–22.

Covey, S. R. (1989). *The seven habits of highly effective people: Restoring the character ethic.* New York: Simon & Schuster.

Craig, S. B., & Gustafson, S. B. (1998). Perceived leader integrity scale: An instrument for assessing employee perceptions of leader integrity. *The Leadership Quarterly, 9,* 127–145.

Crossan, M., Lane, H., & White, R. (1999). An organizational learning framework: From intuition to institution. *Academy of Management Review, 24,* 522–538.

Cummings, L. L., & Schwab, D. P. (1978). Designing appraisal systems for information yield. *California Management Review, 20*(4), 18–25.

Daft, R. L. (2002). *The leadership experience* (2nd ed.). Mason, OH: South-Western.

Daft, R. L. (2005). *The leadership experience* (3rd ed.). Cincinnati, OH: South-Western.

Dalton, J. C. (1999, March). Between the lines: The hard truth about open-book management. *CFO*, pp. 58–64.

Davis, J. H., Schoorman, F. D., & Donaldson, L. (1997). Toward a stewardship theory of management. *Academy of Management Review, 22*, 20–47.

Dean, J. W., Jr., Brandes, P., & Dharwadkar, R. (1998). Organizational cynicism. *Academy of Management Review, 23*(2), 341–352.

Denison, D. R., & Mishra, A. K. (1995). Toward a theory of organizational culture and effectiveness. *Organization Science, 6*, 204–223.

DePaulo, B. (1992). Nonverbal behavior and self-presentation. *Psychological Bulletin, 111, 2*, 203–243.

Derryberry, D. (1987). Incentive and feedback effects on target detection: A chronometric analysis of Gray's model of temperament. *Personality and Individual Differences, 8*, 855–865.

Deutsch, M. (1961). The face of bargaining. *Operations Research, 9*, 886–897.

De Vito, J. (1993). *Essentials of human communication.* New York: HarperCollins.

Dienesch, R., & Liden, R. (1986). Leader-member exchange model of leadership: A critique and further development. *Academy of Management Review, 11*, 618–634.

Diller, B. (1995, November). The discomfort zone. *Inc.*, pp. 19–20.

Dotlich, D. L., & Cairo, P. C. (1999). *Action coaching: How to leverage individual performance for company success.* San Francisco: Jossey-Bass.

Eagly, A. H., & Johnson, B. T. (1990). Gender and leadership style: A meta-analysis. *Psychological Bulletin, 108*, 233–256.

Eagly, A. H., & Karau, S. (2002). Role congruity theory of prejudice toward female leaders. *Psychological Review, 109*, 573–598.

Eagly, A. H., Makhijani, M. G., & Klonsky, B. G. (1992). Gender and the evaluation of leaders: A meta-analysis. *Psychological Bulletin, 111*(3), 22.

Eden, D. (1984). Self-fulfilling prophecy as a managerial tool: Harnessing Pygmalion. *Academy of Management Review, 9*, 64–73.

Eden, D. (1990). *Pygmalion in management: Productivity as a self-fulfilling prophecy.* Lexington, MA: Lexington Books.

Eden, D., Geller, D., Gewirtz, A., Gordon-Terner, R., Inbar, I., Liberman, M., et al. (2000). Implanting pygmalion leadership style through workshop training: Seven field experiments. *The Leadership Quarterly, 11*, 171–210.

Elman, D., Schulte, D., & Buckoff, A. (1977). Effects of facial expression and stare duration on walking speed: Two field experiments. *Environmental Psychology and Nonverbal Behavior, 2*, 93–99.

Emrich, C. G., Denmark, F. L., & Den Hartog, D. N. (2004). Cross-cultural differences in gender egalitarianism: Implications for societies, organizations, and leaders. In R. J. House, P. J. Hanges, M. Javidan, P. W. Dorfman, V. Gupta, & GLOBE Associates (Eds.), *Culture, leadership, and organizations: The GLOBE study of 62 cultures*, 343–394. Thousand Oaks, CA: Sage.

Ettorre, B. (1997). How to get the unvarnished truth. *HR Focus, 74*(8), 1, 4–5.

Fama, E., & Jensen, M. (1983). Agency problems and residual claims. *Journal of Law and Economics, 26*, 301–325.

Fedor, D. B. (1991). Recipient responses to performance feedback: A proposed model and its implications. *Research in Personnel and Human Resources Management, 9*, 73–120.

Fedor, D. B., Davis, W. D., Maslyn, J. M., & Mathieson, K. (2001). Performance improvement efforts in response to negative feedback: The roles of source power and recipient self-esteem. *Journal of Management, 27*, 79–97.

Fehr, B., Baldwin, M., Collins, L., Patterson, S., & Benditt, R. (1999). Anger in close relationships: An interpersonal script analysis. *Personality and Social Psychology Bulletin, 25*, 299–312.

Ferrell, D., & Rusbult, C. (1992). Exploring the exit, voice, loyalty and neglect typology. The influence of job satisfaction, quality of alternatives and investment size. *Employee Responsibilities and Rights Journal, 5*, 201–218.

Fishman, C. (1996, April–May). Whole Foods teams. *Fast Company*, p. 106.

Fiske, S. T., & Taylor, S. E. (1991). *Social cognition*. New York: McGraw-Hill.

Friedrich, P., Mesquita, L., & Hatum, A. (2005). The meaning of difference: Beyond cultural and managerial homogeneity stereotypes of Latin America. *Management Research, 4*(1), 53–71.

Geddes, D., & Baron, R. (1997). Workplace aggression as a consequence of negative performance feedback. *Management Communication Quarterly, 10*, 433–454.

Geddes, D., & Konrad, A. M. (2003). Demographic differences and reactions to performance feedback. *Human Relations, 55*, 1485–1513.

Gelfand, M. J., Bhawuk, D. P., Nishii, L., & Bechtold, D. (2004). Individualism and collectivism. In R. J. House, P. J. Hanges, M. Javidan, P. W. Dorfman, V. Gupta, & GLOBE Associates (Eds.), *Culture, leadership, and organizations: The GLOBE study of 62 cultures*, 438–512. Thousand Oaks, CA: Sage.

Gerstner, C. R., & Day, D. V. (1997). Meta-analysis review of leader-member exchange theory: Correlation and construct issues. *Journal of Applied Psychology, 82*, 827–844.

Ghoshal, S. (2005). Bad management theories are destroying good management practices. *Academy of Management Executive, 4*, 75–91.

Gibson, C. (1997). Do you hear what I hear? A framework for reconciling intercultural communication difficulties arising from cognitive styles and cultural values. In C. Earley & M. Erez (Eds.), *New perspectives on international industrial/organizational psychology*, 335–362. San Francisco: New Lexington.

Goffman, E. (1955). On face-work: An analysis of ritual elements in social interaction. *Psychiatry: Journal for the Study of International Processes, 18*, 213–231.

Gottlieb, J. Z., & Sanzgiri, J. (1996). Towards an ethical dimension of decision making in organizations. *Journal of Business Ethics, 15*, 1275–1285.

Graen, G. B., & Uhl-Bien, M. (1995). Development of leader-member exchange (LMX) theory of leadership over 25 years: Applying a multilevel multi-domain perspective. *The Leadership Quarterly, 6*, 219–247.

Graen, G. B., Wakabayashi, M., Graen, M. R., & Graen, M. G. (1990). International generalizability of American hypotheses about Japanese management progress: A strong inference investigation. *The Leadership Quarterly, 1*, 1–24.

Green, T., & Knippen, J. (1999). *Breaking the barrier to upward communication.* Westport, CT: Quorum Books.

Greer, C. R., & Labig, C. E., Jr. (1987). Employee reactions to disciplinary action. *Human Relations, 40*, 507–524.

Grover, S. L. (1993). Lying, deceit, and subterfuge: A model of dishonesty in the workplace. *Organizational Science, 4*, 478–495.

Gudykunst, W. B., Ting-Toomey, S., & Chua, E. (1988). *Cultural and interpersonal communication.* Newbury Park, CA: Sage.

Gutek, V. A., & Cohen, A. (1987). Sex ratios, sex role spillover and sex at work: A comparison of men's and women's experiences. *Human Relations, 40*, 97–115.

Guthrie, V. A., & Kelly-Radford, L. (1998). Feedback-intensive programs. In C. D. McCauley, R. S. Moxley, & E. Van Velsor (Eds.), *Center for Creative Leadership handbook of leadership development* (pp. 66–105). San Francisco: Jossey-Bass.

Hall, D. T., Otazo, K. L., & Hollenbeck, G. P. (1999, Winter). Behind closed doors: What really happens in executive coaching. *Organizational Dynamics, 29*, 39–53.

Hall, E. (1966). *The hidden dimension.* Garden City, NY: Doubleday.

Hall, E. T. (1976). *Beyond culture.* New York: Doubleday.

Hall, E. T., & Hall, M. R. (1989). *Understanding cultural differences: German, French and American.* Yarmouth, ME: Intercultural Press.

Hallowell, E. M. (1999, January–February). The human moment at work. *Harvard Business Review, 78*, 58–66.

Harackiewicz, J. M., & Manderlink, G. (1984). A process analysis of the effects of performance contingent rewards on intrinsic motivation. *Journal of Experimental Social Psychology, 20*, 531–551.

Heider, F. (1958). *The psychology of interpersonal relations.* New York: Wiley.

Heilman, M. E. (1983). Sex bias in work settings: The lack of fit model. *Research in Organizational Behavior, 5*, 296–298.

Hofstede, G. (1980). *Culture's consequences: International differences in work-related values.* Beverly Hills, CA: Sage.

Hofstede, G. (2001). *Culture's consequences: Comparing values, behaviors, institutions and organizations across nations.* Thousand Oaks, CA: Sage.

Hogan, R., Curphy, G. J., & Hogan, J. (1994). What we know about leadership effectiveness and personality. *American Psychologist, 49*, 493–504.

Hogg, M. A. (2001a). Social identification, group prototypicality, and emergent leadership. In M. A. Hogg & D. J. Terry (Eds.), *Social identity processes in organizational contexts* (pp. 197–212). Philadelphia: Psychology Press.

Hogg, M. A. (2001b). A social identity theory of leadership. *Personality and Social Psychology Review, 5*, 184–200.

Hogg, M. A., Hains, S. C., & Mason, I. (1998). Identification and leadership in small groups: Salience, frame of reference, and leader stereotypicality effects on leader evaluations. *Journal of Personality and Social Psychology, 75*, 1248–1263.

Hoschschild, A. (1983). *The managed heart: Commercialization of human feeling.* Berkeley: University of California Press.

House, R. J., Hanges, P. M., Javidan, M., Dorfman, P., & Gupta, V. (2004). *Culture, leadership and organizations: The GLOBE study of 62 societies.* Thousand Oaks, CA: Sage.

House, R. J., & Howell, J. M. (1992). Personality and charismatic leadership. *The Leadership Quarterly, 3*, 81–108.

Housel, T., & Davis, W. (1977). The reduction of upward communication distortion. *The Journal of Business Communication, 14*(4), 49–65.

Howard, A., & Bray, D. W. (1988). *Managerial lives in transition: Advancing age and changing times.* New York: Guilford.

Howard, R. A. (1992). Business ethics: Tell the truth. *Journal of Management Development, 11*, 4–10.

Hwang, K. (1987). Face and favor: The Chinese power game. *American Journal of Sociology, 92*, 944–974.

Ilgen, D. R., & Davis, C. (2000). Bearing bad news: Reactions to negative performance feedback. *Applied Psychology: An International Review, 49*, 550–565.

Ilgen, D. R., & Feldman, J. (1983). Performance appraisal: A process focus. *Research in Organizational Behavior, 5*, 141–197.

Ilgen, D. R., Fisher, C. D., & Taylor, M. S. (1979). Consequences of individual feedback on behavior in organizations. *Journal of Applied Psychology, 64*, 349–371.

Ilgen, D. R., Mitchell, T. R., & Frederickson, J. W. (1981). Poor performance: Supervisors' and subordinates' responses. *Organizational Behavior and Human Performance, 27*, 386–410.

Jaworski, B. J., & Kohli, A. K. (1991). Supervisory feedback: Alternative types and their impact on salespeople's performance and satisfaction. *Journal of Marketing Research, 28*, 190–201.

Jensen, M. (2001). Value maximization, stakeholder theory, and the corporate objective function. *European Financial Management, 7*, 297–317.

Jensen, M., & Meckling, W. (1976). Theory of the firm: Managerial behavior, agency costs and ownership structure. *Journal of Financial Economics, 3*, 305–360.

Judge, T. A., & Piccolo, R. F. (2004). Transformational and transactional leadership: A meta-analytic test of their relative validity. *Journal of Applied Psychology, 89*, 755–768.

Kanfer, R., & Ackerman, P. L. (1989). Motivation and cognitive abilities: An integration/aptitude-treatment interaction approach to skill acquisition. *Journal of Applied Psychology, 74*, 657–690.

Kassing, J., & Armstrong, T. (2002). Someone's going to hear about this. *Management Communication Quarterly, 16*, 39–65.

Katz, D., & Kahn, R. L. (1978). *The social psychology of organizations* (2nd ed.). New York: Wiley.

Keating, C. (1985). Human dominance signals: The primate in us. In S. L. Ellyson & J. F. Dovido (Eds.), *Power, dominance and nonverbal behavior* (pp. 89–108). New York: Springer-Verlag.

Kelley, R. E. (1992). *The power of followership.* New York: Doubleday.

Kernis, M. H., & Sun, C. (1994). Narcissism and reactions to interpersonal feedback. *Journal of Research in Personality, 28*, 4–13.

Kets de Vries, M. F. R. (1993). *Leaders, fools, and imposters.* San Francisco: Jossey-Bass.

Kierstead, D., D'Agostino, P., & Dill, H. (1988). Sex role stereotyping of college professors: Bias in students' ratings of instructor. *Journal of Educational Psychology*, 80, 342–344.

Kimble, C., & Helmreich, R. (1972). Self-esteem and the need for social approval. *Psychonomic Science, 26*, 239–242.

Klimoski, R., & Mohammed, S. (1994). Team mental model: Construct or metaphor? *Journal of Management, 20*, 403–437.

Kluger, A. N., & DeNisi, A. (1996). The effects of feedback interventions on performance: A historical review, a meta-analysis, and a preliminary feedback theory. *Psychological Bulletin, 119*, 254–284.

Korsgaard, A. (1996). The impact of self-appraisals on reactions to feedback from others. *Journal of Organizational Behavior, 17*, 301–311.

Kotter, J. P., & Heskett, J. L. (1992). *Corporate culture and performance*. New York: Free Press.

La France, M., Hecht, M., & Paluck, E. (2003). The contingent smile: A meta-analysis of sex differences in smiling. *Psychological Bulletin, 129*, 2, 305–334.

Larson, J. (1984). The performance feedback process: A preliminary model. *Organizational Behavior and Human Performance, 33*, 42–76.

Larson, J. (1986). Supervisors' performance feedback to subordinates: The role of subordinate performance valence and outcome dependence. *Organizational Behavior and Human Decision Processes, 37*, 391–408.

Larson, J. (1989). The dynamic interplay between employees' feedback-seeking strategies and supervisors' delivery of performance feedback. *Academy of Management Review, 14*, 408–422.

Latting, J. K. (1992). Giving corrective feedback: A decisional analysis. *Social Work, 37*, 424–430.

Leana, C. R., Locke, E. A., & Schweiger, D. M. (1990). Fact and fiction in analyzing research on participative decision-making: A critique of Cotton, Vollrath, Froggatt, Lengnick-Hall, and Jennings. *Academy of Management Review, 15*, 137–146.

Leathers, D. (1992). *Successful nonverbal communication: Principles and applications*. NY: McMillan.

Leung, K., Su, S., & Morris, M. W. (2001). When is criticism not constructive? The roles of fairness perceptions and dispositional attributions in employee acceptance of critical supervisory feedback. *Human Relations, 54*, 1155–1187.

Level, D., & Galle, W. (1988). *Managerial communications*. Plano, TX: Business Publications.

Levine, D. (1985). *The flight from ambiguity*. Chicago: University of Chicago Press.

Light, D. A. (2001, January). Who goes, who stays? *Harvard Business Review*, 35–44.

Lizzio, A., Wilson, K., Gilchrist, J., & Gallois, C. (2003). The role of gender in the construction and evaluation of feedback effectiveness. *Management Communication Quarterly, 16*, 341–379.

London, M. (2001). The great debate: Should multisource feedback be used for administration or development only? In D. Bracken, C. W. Timmereck, & A. Church (Eds.), *Handbook of multisource feedback*, 368–385. San Francisco: Jossey-Bass.

London, M. (2003). *Job feedback: Giving, seeking, and using feedback for performance improvement* (2nd ed.). Mahwah, NJ: Lawrence Erlbaum Associates, Inc.

Lord, R. G., Foti, R. J., & DeVader, C. L. (1984). A test of leadership categorization theory: Internal structure, information processing, and leadership perceptions. *Organizational Behavior and Human Performance, 34,* 343–378.

Lord, R. G., & Maher, K. J. (1991). *Leadership and information processing: Linking perceptions and performance.* Boston: Unwin-Hyman.

Lowe, K. B., Kroeck, K. G., & Sivasubramaniam, N. (1996). Effectiveness correlates of transformational and transactional leadership: A meta-analytic review of the MLQ literature. *The Leadership Quarterly, 7,* 385–425.

Lubatkin, M., Schweiger, D., & Weber, Y. (1999). Top management turnover in related M&A's: An additional test of the theory of relative standing. *Journal of Management, 25,* 55–73.

Maccoby, M. (2004, January). Narcissistic leaders: The incredible pros, the inevitable cons. *Harvard Business Review, 82,* 92–101.

March, J. (1991). Exploration and exploitation in organizational learning. *Organization Science, 2,* 71–87.

Marks, M. L., & Mirvis, P. H. (1998). *Joining forces: Making one plus one equal three in mergers, acquisitions, and alliances.* San Francisco: Jossey-Bass.

Martin, M. M. (1998). Trust leadership. *Journal of Leadership Studies, 5*(3), 41–49.

McCarty, P. (1986). Effects of feedback on the self-confidence of men and women. *Academy of Management Journal, 29,* 840–847.

McClelland, D. C. (1985). *Human motivation.* Glenview, IL: Scott Foresman.

McClelland, D. C., & Boyatzis, R. E. (1982). Leadership motive pattern and long-term success in management. *Journal of Applied Psychology, 67,* 737–743.

McCune, J. C. (1998, July–August). That elusive thing called trust. *Management Review,* pp. 10–16.

McDonald, P., & Gandz, J. (1992). Getting value from shared values. *Organizational Dynamics, 21*(3), 64–76.

McFarland, C., & Miller, D. T. (1994). The framing of relative performance feedback: Seeing the glass as half empty or half full. *Journal of Personality and Social Psychology, 66,* 1061–1073.

McFarlin, D. B., & Blascovich, J. (1981). Effects of self-esteem and performance feedback on future affective preferences and cognitive expectations. *Journal of Personality and Social Psychology, 40,* 521–531.

McGregor, D. (1960). *The human side of enterprise.* New York: McGraw-Hill.

McGregor, D. (2006). *The human side of enterprise* (Updated ed.). New York: McGraw-Hill.

McKnight, D., Cummings, L., & Chervany, N. (1998). Initial trust formation in new organizational relationships. *Academy of Management Review, 23,* 473–490.

Mehrabian, A. (1981). *Silent messages: Implicit communication of emotions and attitudes* (2nd ed.). Belmont, CA: Wadsworth.

Miller, D. T., & Vidmar, N. (1981). The social psychology of punishment reactions. In M. J. Lerner & S. C. Lerner (Eds.), *The justice motive in social behavior* (pp. 145–168). New York: Plenum.

Miner, J. B. (1975). The uncertain future of the leadership concept: An overview. In J. G. Hunt & L. L. Larson (Eds.), *Leadership frontiers*. Kent, OH: Kent State University Press.

Mintzberg, H. (1973). *The nature of managerial work*. New York: Harper & Row.

Mirvis, P., & Kanter, D. (1991). Beyond demography: A psychographic profile of the workforce. *Human Resource Management, 30*, 45–68.

Morosini, P. (1998). *Managing cultural differences: Effective strategy and execution across cultures in global corporate alliances*. New York: Elsevier.

Moss, S. E., & Sanchez, J. I. (2004). Are your employees avoiding you? Managerial strategies for closing the feedback gap. *Academy of Management Executive, 18*(1), 32–44.

Munchus, G., III, & McArthur, B. (1991). Revisiting the historical use of the assessment center in management selection and development. *Journal of Management Development, 10*, 5–13.

Nanus, B. (1992). *Visionary leadership*. San Francisco: Jossey-Bass.

Nemeroff, W., & Wexley, K. (1977). Relationships between performance appraisal characteristics and interview outcomes as perceived by supervisors and subordinates. *Proceedings of the Academy of Management, 30*–34.

Okabe, R. (1983). Cultural assumptions of East and West: Japan and the United States. In W. Gudykunst (Ed.), *Intercultural communication theory*, 21–44. Beverly Hills, CA: Sage.

Parry, K. W., & Proctor-Thomson, S. B. (2002). Perceived integrity of transformational leaders in organizational settings. *Journal of Business Ethics, 35*, 75–96.

Patterson, C. M., Kosson, D. S., & Newman, J. P. (1987). Reaction to punishment, reflectivity, and passive avoidance learning in extraverts. *Journal of Personality and Social Psychology, 52*, 565–575.

Pearce, C. L., & Conger, J. A. (2003). All those years ago: The historical underpinnings of shared leadership. In C. L. Pearce & J. A. Conger (Eds.), *Shared leadership: Reframing the hows and whys of leadership* (pp. 1–18). Thousand Oaks, CA: Sage.

Pearce-McCall, D. N., & Newman, J. P. (1986). Expectation of success following noncontingent punishment in introverts and extraverts. *Journal of Personality and Social Psychology, 50*, 439–446.

Pease, A. (1984). *Signals: How to use body language for power, success and love*. New York: Bantam.

Peters, T. (1987). *Thriving on chaos*. New York: Harper Perennial.

Peterson, D. (1983). Conflict. In H. H. Kelley, E. Berscheid, A. Christensen, J. Harvey, T. Huston, G. Levinger, et al. (Eds.), *Close relationships* (pp. 360–396). New York: Freeman.

Pfeffer, J., & Veiga, J. F. (1999). Putting people first for organizational success. *Academy of Management Executive, 13*(2), 37–48.

Pillai, R., Scandura, T., & Williams, E. (1999). Leadership and organizational justice: Similarities and differences across cultures. *Journal of International Business Studies, 30*, 763–779.

Podsakoff, P. M., & Farh, J. L. (1989). Effects of feedback sign and credibility on goal setting and task performance. *Organizational Behavior and Human Decision Processes, 44*, 45–67.

Podsakoff, P., MacKenzie, S., Moorman, R., & Fetter, R. (1990). Transformational leader behaviors and their effects on followers' trust in leader, satisfaction, and organizational citizenship behaviors. *The Leadership Quarterly, 1*, 107–142.

Poe, A. C. (2003, July). Don't touch that "send" button! *HR Magazine*, pp. 74–80.

Polzer, J. T., Milton, L. P., & Swann, W. B., Jr. (2002). Capitalizing on diversity: Interpersonal congruence in small work groups. *Administrative Science Quarterly, 47*, 296–324.

Pruitt, D. G. (1998). Social conflict. In D. T. Gilbert, S. T. Fiske, & G. Lindzey (Eds.), *The handbook of social psychology* (pp. 470–503). New York: McGraw-Hill.

Rakos, R. F. (1991). *Assertive behavior: Theory, research and training.* London: Routledge.

Reichers, A. E., Wanous, J. P., & Austin, J. T. (1997). Understanding and managing cynicism about organizational change. *Academy of Management Executive, 11*(1), 48–59.

Rose, D. S., & Farrell, T. (2002). *The use and abuse of comments in 360-degree feedback* (3D Group Tech. Rep. No. 8118). Berkeley, CA: Data Driven Decisions.

Rosener, J. B. (1997). *America's competitive secret: Women managers.* New York: Oxford University Press.

Rudawsky, D. J., Lundgren, D. C., & Grasha, A. F. (1999). Competitive and collaborative responses to negative feedback. *International Journal of Conflict Management, 10*, 172–190.

Rue, L., & Byars, L. (1995). *Management skills and application* (7th ed.). Chicago: Irwin.

Rumelhart, D. E. (1984). Schemata and the cognitive system. In R. S. Wyer & T. K. Srull (Eds.), *The handbook of social cognition* (Vol. 1, pp. 161–188). Hillsdale, NJ: Lawrence Erlbaum Associates, Inc.

Sager, I., & Brady, D. (1999, June 14). Big Blue's Blunt Bohemian. *Business Week*, pp. 107–112.

Sagie, A. (1997). Leader direction and employee participation in decision making: Contradictory or compatible practices. *Applied Psychology: An International Review, 46*, 387–452.

Sagrestano, L. M. (1992). Power strategies in interpersonal relationships: The effects of expertise and gender. *Psychology of Women Quarterly, 16*, 481–495.

Schein, E. H. (2004). Learning when and how to lie: A neglected aspect of organizational and occupational socialization. *Human Relations, 57*, 260–273.

Schlenker, B. R. (1980). *Impression management: The self-concept, social identity, and interpersonal relations.* Monterey, CA: Brooks/Cole.

Schweiger, D. M., & DeNisi, A. S. (1991). Communication with employees following a merger: A longitudinal field experiment. *Academy of Management Journal, 34*, 110–135.

Seifert, C., Yukl, G., & McDonald, R. (2003). Effects of multisource feedback and a feedback facilitator on the influence behavior of managers toward subordinates. *Journal of Applied Psychology, 88*, 561–569.

Sendjaya, S., & Sarros, J. C. (2002). Servant leadership: Its origin, development, and application in organizations. *Journal of Leadership and Organizational Studies, 9*(2), 57–64.

Senge, P. M. (1990). *The fifth discipline: The art and practice of the learning organization*. New York: Doubleday.

Shen, W. (2003). The dynamics of the CEO-board relationship: An evolutionary perspective. *Academy of Management Review, 28,* 466–476.

Sherony, K. M., & Green, S. G. (2002). Coworker exchange: Relationships between coworkers, leader-member exchange and work attitudes. *Journal of Applied Psychology, 87,* 542–548.

Silver, M., Conte, R., Miceli, M., & Poggi, I. (1986). Humiliation: Feeling social control, and the construction of reality. *Journal of the Theory of Social Behavior, 16,* 269–283.

Silver, W. S., Mitchell, T. R., & Gist, M. E. (1995). Responses to successful and unsuccessful performance: The moderating effect of self-efficacy on the relationship between performance and attributions. *Organizational Behavior and Human Decision Processes, 62,* 286–299.

Sims, R. L. (2002). Support for the use of deception within the work environment: A comparison of Israeli and U.S. employee attitudes. *Journal of Business Ethics, 35,* 27–34.

Smither, J., London, M., Flautt, R., Vargas, Y., & Kucine, I. (2002, April). *Does discussing multisource feedback with raters enhance performance improvement?* Paper presented at the 17th annual conference of the Society for Industrial and Organizational Psychology, Toronto.

Smither, J. W., & Reilly, S. P. (2001). Coaching in organizations. In M. London (Ed.), *How people evaluate others in organizations* (pp. 221–252). Mahwah, NJ: Lawrence Erlbaum Associates, Inc.

Spector, P. E. (2002). Employee control and occupational stress. *American Psychological Society, 11,* 153–156.

Spence, J. T., & Helmreich, R. L. (1983). Achievement related motives and behaviors. In J. T. Spence (Ed.), *Achievement and achievement motives: Psychological and sociological perspectives* (pp. 7–74). San Francisco: Freeman.

Stajkovic, A. D., & Luthans, F. (1998). Self-efficacy and work-related performance: A meta-analysis. *Psychological Bulletin, 124,* 240–261.

Steele, F. (1975). *The open organization: The impact of secrecy and disclosure on people and organizations*. Reading, MA: Addison-Wesley.

Stevens, G. E., & DeNisi, A. S. (1980). Women as managers: Attitudes and attributions for performance by men and women. *Academy of Management Journal, 23,* 355–361.

Stipek, D., Weiner, B., & Li, K. (1989). Testing some attribution-emotion relations in the People's Republic of China. *Journal of Personality and Social Psychology, 56,* 109–116.

Stone, D. L., Gueutal, H. G., & McIntosh, B. (1984). The effects of feedback sequence and expertise of the rater on perceived feedback accuracy. *Personnel Psychology, 37,* 487–506.

Stull, J. B. (1988). Giving feedback to foreign-born employees. *Management Solutions, 33*(7), 42.

Sully, M., Waldman, D. A., Washburn, N., & House, R. J. (2006). *Unrequited profits: Evidence for the stakeholder perspective*. Unpublished manuscript.

Swan, W., & Margulies, P. (1991). *How to do a superior performance appraisal*. New York: Wiley.

Sweetland, S. R., & Hoy, W. K. (2001). Varnishing the truth in schools: Principals and teachers spinning reality. *Journal of Educational Administration, 39,* 282–293.

Tata, J. (2002). The influence of managerial accounts on employees' reactions to negative feedback. *Group and Organization Management, 27,* 480–503.

Thomas, T., Schermerhorn, J. R., Jr., & Dienhart, J. W. (2004). Strategic leadership of ethical behavior in business. *Academy of Management Executive, 18*(2), 56–66.

Thompson, S. C. (1981). Will it hurt less if I can control it? A complex answer to a simple question. *Psychological Bulletin, 90,* 89–101.

Thorndike, E. (1927). The law of effect. *American Journal of Psychology, 39,* 212–222.

Thornton, G. C., III, & Cleveland, J. N. (1990). Developing managerial talent through simulation. *American Psychologist, 45,* 190–199.

Tiggemann, M., Winefield, A. H., & Brebner, J. (1982). The role of extraversion in the development of learned helplessness. *Personality and Individual Differences, 3,* 27–34.

VandeWalle, D., Cron, W., & Slocum, J. (2001). The role of goal orientation following performance feedback. *Journal of Applied Psychology, 86,* 629–640.

Van Velsor, E., & Leslie, J. B. (1995). Why executives derail: Perspective across time and cultures. *Academy of Management Executive, 9*(4), 62–72.

Vecchio, R. P., Bullis, R. C., & Brazil, D. M. (2006). The utility of situational leadership theory: A replication in a military setting. *Small Group Research, 37,* 407–424.

Veiga, J. F. (1988). Face your problem subordinates now. *Academy of Management Executive, 2,* 145–152.

Vera, D., & Crossan, M. (2004). Strategic leadership and organizational learning. *Academy of Management Review, 29,* 222–240.

Vidmar, N. (1974). Retributive and utilitarian motives and other correlates of Canadian attitudes toward the death penalty. *The Canadian Psychologist, 15,* 337–356.

Vidmar, N., & Crinklaw, L. (1974). Attributing responsibility for an accident: A methodological and conceptual critique. *Canadian Journal of Behavioral Science, 6,* 112–130.

Vroom, V. H. (2000). Leadership and the decision-making process. *Organizational Dynamics, 28*(4), 82–94.

Vroom, V. H., & Jago, A. G. (1988). *The new leadership: Managing participation in organizations.* Englewood Cliffs, NJ: Prentice-Hall.

Vroom, V. H., & Jago, A. G. (1995). Situation effects and levels of analysis in the study of leader participation. *The Leadership Quarterly, 6,* 169–181.

Waldersee, R., & Luthans, F. (1994). The impact of positive and corrective feedback on customer service performance: Summary. *Journal of Organizational Behavior, 15,* 84–95.

Waldman, D. A., & Atwater, L. E. (2001). Confronting barriers to successful implementation of multisource feedback. In D. W. Bracken, C. W. Timmreck, & A. H. Church (Eds.), *The handbook of multisource feedback: The comprehensive resource for designing and implementing MSF processes* (pp. 463–477). San Francisco: Jossey-Bass.

Waldman, D. A., Atwater, L. E., & Antonioni, D. (1998). Has 360-degree feedback gone amok? *Academy of Management Executive, 12*(2), 86–94.

Waldman, D. A., & Korbar, T. (2004). Student assessment center performance in the prediction of early career success. *Academy of Management Learning and Education, 3,* 151–167.

Waldman, D. A., Sully, M., Washburn, N., House, R. J., Adetoun, B., Barrasa, A., et al. (2006). Cultural and leadership predictors of corporate social responsibility values of top management: A GLOBE study of 15 countries. *Journal of International Business Studies, 37,* 823–837.

Walker, A. G., & Smither, J. W. (1999). A five-year study of upward feedback: What managers do with their results matters. *Personnel Psychology, 52,* 393–423.

Wilson, K. L., & Gallois, C. (1993). *Assertion and its social context.* Elmsford, NY: Pergamon.

Winter, D. G. (1991). A motivational model of leadership: Predicting long-term management success from TAT measures of power motivation and responsibility. *The Leadership Quarterly, 2,* 67–80.

Yammarino, F., & Atwater, L. (1993). Understanding self-perception accuracy: Implications for human resources management. *Human Resource Management, 32,* 231–247.

Yukl, G. (1998). *Leadership in organizations* (4th ed.). Upper Saddle River, NJ: Prentice-Hall.

Yukl, G. (2002). *Leadership in organizations* (5th ed.). Upper Saddle River, NJ: Prentice-Hall.

Yukl, G. (2006). *Leadership in organizations* (6th ed.). Upper Saddle River, NJ: Prentice-Hall.

Zaremba, A. (1993). *Management in a new key: Communication in the modern organization.* Norcross, GA: Institute of Industrial Engineers.

Zhou, J. (1998). Feedback valence, feedback style, task autonomy, and achievement orientation: Interactive effects on creative performance. *Journal of Applied Psychology, 83,* 261–276.

Subject Index

Author Index

A

Ackerman, P. L., 54, 144
Adetoun, B., 94, 96, 151
Adler, N. J., 28, 29, 137
Ahrens, A. H., 37, 137
Allen, J. B., 42, 140
Alloy, L. B., 37, 137
Andersen, P., 73, 137
Antonioni, D., 129, 130, 150
Armstrong, T., 45, 144
Arvey, R. D., 20, 137
Ashford, S., 4, 137
Ashford, S. J., 23, 84, 137
Atkinson, J. W., 37, 137
Atwater, D., 50, 115, 138
Atwater, L., 40, 43, 60, 124, 138,
        140, 151
Atwater, L. E., 3, 13–15, 18, 19, 24,
        41, 42, 50, 54, 55, 63–65,
        115, 129, 130, 138, 140, 150
Austin, J. T., 115, 148
Avolio, B. J., 23, 94, 138, 139

B

Bailey, J. R., 29, 138
Baldwin, M., 14, 142
Bandura, A., 15, 17, 18, 20, 138
Baron, R., 13, 142
Baron, R. A., 17, 46, 63, 138
Barrasa, A., 94, 96, 151
Bass, B. M., 21, 23, 94, 124, 139
Baumeister, R., 15, 139

Bechtold, D., 28, 29, 142
Beebe, S., 71, 139
Benditt, R., 14, 142
Benedict, M. E., 24, 139
Bennis, W., 120, 139
Berson, Y., 116, 139
Bhawuk, D. P., 28, 29, 142
Birdwhistell, R., 71, 139
Blanchard, K., 128, 139
Blascovich, J., 15, 146
Block, P., 93, 139
Boddy, J., 38, 139
Boehm, V. R., 36, 139
Bond, M., 33, 139
Boyatzis, R. E., 108, 146
Bracken, D., 53, 139
Bracken, D. W., 53, 139
Brady, D., 125, 148
Brandes, P., 115, 141
Bray, D. W., 127, 144
Brazil, D. M., 91, 97, 150
Brebner, J., 38, 150
Brenner, O. C., 40, 139
Brett, J., 40, 43, 138
Brett, J. F., 14, 18, 19, 42, 54, 55, 64,
        129, 138, 140
Brown, J. D., 19, 37, 140
Buck, R., 75, 140
Buckoff, A., 76, 141
Bullis, R. C., 91, 97, 150
Burke, R., 64, 140
Butler, J., 98, 140
Byars, L., 45, 148

HD 57.7 .A83 2008

Atwater, Leanne E.

Leadership, feedback, and
the open communication gap